ALLENGINSBERG
INAMERICA

JANE KRAMER

ALLEN GINSBERG IN AMERICA

WITH A NEW INTRODUCTION BY THE AUTHOR

FROMM INTERNATIONAL PUBLISHING CORPORATION
NEW YORK

First Fromm International Paperback, 1997

Copyright © Jane Kramer 1968, 1969, 1997

All rights reserved under International and Pan-American Copyright Conventions. Published in the United States by Fromm International Publishing Corporation, New York. First published by Random House, Inc., New York, in 1969

LIBRARY OF CONGRESS CATALOGING-IN-PUBLICATION DATA

Kramer, Jane.
  Allen Ginsberg in America / Jane Kramer.
    p. cm.
  Originally published: New York : Random House, 1969.
  ISBN 0-88064-189-4
  1. Ginsberg, Allen, 1926– —Biography. 2. Poets, American—20th century—Biography. I. Title
  PS3513.I74Z73 1997
  811'.54—dc21
  [B]   97-21425
                                                     CIP

10 9 8 7 6 5 4 3 2 1

Manufactured in the United States of America

ACKNOWLEDGMENTS

My thanks and appreciation to William Shawn and *The New Yorker*, John J. Simon, Sandy Campbell, Jessie Kramer, Heenie Fineman, Judith and Jeremy Ets-Hokin, and to all the friends and relatives of Allen Ginsberg, who were also of enormous help to me.

To Allen

Introduction

The news came this way: "Allen died." It was a Saturday morning last April, and I can't believe that anyone who picked up the phone and heard those two words, as I did many times that morning, had any doubt who "Allen" was. When Allen Ginsberg came into your life he settled there—intimate, indispensable, and so familiar you could not imagine your life before him. It didn't matter if you had heard him read once, as a student, or were a lover or an old, close friend; it didn't matter if you lived halfway around the world from Allen or kept a toothbrush in his Manhattan flat. Allen belonged to the person you were, or hoped you were, or liked to think you could be.

Forty years ago, when Allen's mother wrote the letter that he quotes in "Kaddish," she told Allen: "The key is in the window, the key is in the sunlight in the window—I have the key—get married Allen don't take drugs." And while Naomi Ginsberg was mad and dying when she wrote that letter, she really did have, I think, the key to Allen. He was a born paterfamilias—nurturer, provider, the proud father of his tribe—which may be why, even now, people persist in calling him "the father of the beat generation" when in fact it is *his* generation they mean. He embraced the world. He thought that with love, sex, a good mantra, and what he called "the right spiritual information," anybody's bad boy could be turned around and put on a path to enlightenment. When I met him, a few years into the Vietnam war, he was trying out his theory in letters to people like Robert MacNamara, telling them to stay calm, telling them that this thing called "enemies" was just a bad dream, something in their heads. He reminded me then of some television Dad, writing his weekly admonishments to a son who's acting up because the boy in the next tent at camp has hurt his feelings.

I actually met Allen through one of the bad boys—a kid named Tommy who had got lost along the path to enlightenment and was helpless and homeless in New York. Tommy had arrived in New York from Nashville three years earlier, carrying a flute and the mothy remains of his father's football-stadium fur coat, all set to apply some Southern charm and salesmanship to what he thought of as his new Aquarian principles. I remember that he once showed up at an editing room at CBS, where I was putting together a documentary, with fifteen dollars worth of tickets to a "Let's Legalize Marijuana" rally in his pocket and managed to unload them all onto a station janitor and four Republicans from the news staff. I remember this becase a few months later he was arrested for selling two pounds of marijuana, tried, convicted on the testimony of an informer posing as a pothead, and then released, pending an appeal. He broke the terms of his first bail bond, and wound up in a cell at the West Street prison until he was released again, in his parents' custody. After a few penitent months at home, he packed a bag and disappeared and eventually turned up, with the police on his trail, back in New York—which is when he appeared at my door, one snowy December night in 1966, wrapped in that old fur coat. He was shivering badly, his teeth were chattering, his eyes were glassy, and from what I could make out he was just starting to come down from a long and ravishing amphetamine high. He said that he had been walking for hours. The four girls who lived in the apartment near Columbia where he had been bunking all week had finally thrown him out, and Tommy had grabbed his coat and started walking downtown. Passing my building, he decided that he wanted soup. I asked him where he was going, because I suspected he might not be going anywhere. Tommy said, "Where else? Allen's house."

For me, in 1966, Allen Ginsberg was the name attached to a couple of poems I liked and to a legend that was more often than not referred to as Allen-Ginsberg-Jack-Kerouac-Gregory-Corso. Allen was the one with the beard, the one who showed up everywhere reading "Howl." In 1966, I had most of the stereotype notions of a worn beatnik, whose poetry was affecting, but whose style of life was bound to be ridiculous. Still, dishing out soup that night, wishing that Tommy would leave and at the same time embarrassed that I was such an unneighborly sort of person, I began to develop a strong, if grudging, curiousity about the poet. Judging from Tommy's condition, it was clear that Allen Ginsberg would be neighborly to just about anyone.

A few days later, I called Allen on the telephone. I was very nervous. Tommy had warned him that I might be calling, and Allen, by chance, had come across an old *Voice* story of mine in an anthology a friend had sent him. Allen announced right away that he hadn't much liked the story, but then he sighed and said, "Well, people change." He also wanted to know if any of the editors I worked with were closet queens—closet queen, coming from Allen, was the ultimate insult—who, because of sneaky qualities of soul, might be tempted to tamper with his persona in my manuscript. Finally, he indulged in some delicate questioning, which he then confessed was prompted by the suspicion that I was a "lady narc." By any ordinary standards, the things he said were either rude, ludicrous, or both, but Allen had managed to make them absolutely friendly. He sounded like a nice man who happened to have a few reasonable misgivings about starting a project with someone from a magazine like *The New Yorker*—which, he pointed out, had never allowed the words "fuck," "vagina," or "blow job" in its pages. We made a date for the next morning. After I hung up, I knew that I liked him already for treating me to such a candid, peculiar conversation.

I arrived at his old apartment, in the East Village, at about eleven. It looked like a cross between an underground newspaper office and a beat hotel. Half a dozen house guests were in the process of waking up—wandering around naked, yawning, blinking, drinking coffee. A visiting San Franciscan, who was going to publish Allen's South American journals, was sitting on a mattress in the front room of the railroad flat, reading copy, and an old girlfriend of Allen's from New Jersey, who had volunteered to set up a cross-referenced card catalogue for his notes and papers, was busy dumping the contents of a metal filing cabinet onto the dining-room floor. There was a lot of noise. Someone in a bedroom was chanting. Allen's television, radio, and portable stereo sets were on. And the girl from New Jersey was listening to a tape of an interview with Allen by a Nebraska housewife. (The housewife was saying, "That's *Howl*, I presume, as in 'howling with laughter.'") Allen himself was perched on top of an old wooden desk near the publisher's mattress, chewing spearmint gumdrops and talking on the phone to Timothy Leary about the marijuana test cases that were due to be scheduled that winter in the federal courts.

The next few months saw the brief, bright heyday of Love in the Haight-Ashbury and Flower Power on the campuses. LSD held promises of becoming, as Allen put it, a "useful educational tool."

The instinct for community was high for the first time, really, since Brook Farm. Tenderness had been taken up by students as the lost chord in the political melody. Satori was enjoying a revival as a kind of all-purpose spiritual spa. ("It's like, if you're a *real* Bodhisattva," Allen was once instructed by a woman in his favorite California sexual commune, "then...ideally you should want to fuck everybody in the universe.") It was a nice moment, but the young casualties of the movement, like Tommy, were beginning to appear.

Allen had an incredible concern for those casualties. There was a good deal of discussion then in Allen's circle about what the proper attitude to them should be, and I remember that some of his more doctrinaire friends, like the poet Gary Snyder—who for a while was Allen's co-adviser to the Haight-Ashbury—argued that casualties were inevitable in times of profound social revolution and that, given their inexorable bad karma, it was useless for the revolution to worry too much about them. Allen, on the other hand, worried. There were always a few lost souls attached to his rotating brood, and he looked after them all—so well, in fact, and so cheerfully, that many of them left his household quite unnerved by the whole experience. Watching Allen with the freak-outs and flip-outs and drop-outs of the late sixties, I began to realize the extent to which what had at first seemed like a full-fledged rescue operation was really just a natural reflex of his own very special strength and sanity. His household worked—and so much of what he was prescribing for the rest of the world seemed eminently workable—largely because Allen himself worked so well as a personality. His household, wherever he happened to put it, was a communal prototype, though very few of the hippies' communes ever measured up to it. Emmet Grogan's San Francisco Diggers, who were around then and for a while considered the last word in togetherness, turned out to be more like an army of buck privates under a temperamental general than a hippie love nest. Most of the sacred-orgy societies, like the California commune, were oppressed by their various "Buddhist" mandates to share everything and everybody. And seekers in the acid conclaves, like Tim Leary's, often ended up preaching relentlessly to one another over fine points of dogma, such as who should do the dishes and how many centigrams, precisely, a true believer needed to consume. By contrast, the ease and open-endedness of life at Allen's was even more remarkable. Too many of his critics—and followers—tended to forget, as I did then, the fact that Allen had put years, and a great deal of anguish, into his own freedom, and that he was a disciplined artist and a thoroughly educated man. He had worked for his mysticism, and it was bound to be different in its tenacity and substance from the quick-vision ecstasy of a runaway fourteen-year-old. I remember a talk in California between Allen and some of his friends in the communal family. One of them announced that with the right amount of LSD a person could save a lot of time getting insights, and he added, "...the old yoga may guarantee that with enough discipline you'll reach certain states of mind and certain experiences, but an acid yoga makes *sure* you have the experience, the actual zap of the experience." Allen listened for a while, and then said: "Just taking acid's no yoga." Finally, he added, "Yoga is getting through acid, knowing what to do with acid. Yoga is knowing how to be *neat* when you're high."

For me, getting to know Allen was such a large, happy experience that months went by before I could piece together some impressions and actually begin writing. (I'm not sure what, exactly, I had expected of Allen, but coming home from our first day together I was astounded by the fact that he had gone to the bank to deposit a check and then slipped into a local diner for some bacon and eggs.) By the time I finished, over a year and a half had passed since the Great Human Be-In in Central Park with which this book ends; Vietnam was more and more on everybody's mind; Be-Ins had given way to campus sieges as the preferred form of communal enterprise; and I myself was living in a small, imperial city in the middle of Morocco, where all the hippies were tourists and where the last student reckless enough to complain about anything was wasting away in jail. The isolation I felt then from war protesters, student activists, hippie lovers, and virtually every other sign of young, revolutionary life was as much spiritual as spatial. It was impossible to imagine Allen Ginsberg in Morocco, and thinking about Allen there, I began to understand how very much he belonged in and to America. Allen was often called a mystic, but despite his exuberant plunges into Eastern disciplines and forms, Allen's was that odd, optimistic, American brand of mysticism which he traced, quite rightly, back to Whitman, and which was rooted in humanism and in a romantic and visionary ideal of harmony amoung human beings. That buoyant humanism, that vision of a felicitous and sexy life-in-the-world, that exceptional tenderness, had nothing whatever to do with the holy men I was encountering in Morocco, where questions of compassion and community and fellow-feeling were considered quite irrelevant to the pursuit of a lively ecstatic life. In America, it had been easy and of course exciting to believe that Allen's vision could take hold and flower anywhere. But I was in a place where a good part of the population spent its time having visions, and there was no appetite at all for Allen's loving universe. By the time I finished writing I was beginning to see, sadly, how much a redeeming vision needs a "community of the enlightened," as the Buddhists say, that is ready to receive it.

Allen once told me that he was "not as nice, not as easy" as my book made him. I think that—being so young then, expecially to Allen's forty-year-old paterfamilias, and so enchanted by the promise of that benign American moment that he represented and, for all intents and purposes, invented—I never really accounted for the cost to Allen of all that buoyancy and all that tenderness and all the syncretizing passion. I was a student of literature; I knew Allen's discipline as a writer and even his discipline as a person, but not really his exhaustion. Allen's father, Louis, who was a Sunday poet, used to shake his head at Allen's wanderings and his errant enthusiasms and say that Allen was "restless." He thought (and in this he was not so different from Allen's mother) that all Allen needed to do was locate himself—in his head, in the world—and Allen would be "cured" of too much seeking. What he missed, of course, was the purpose of Allen's bardic mission. What Allen wanted to cure was America. He wanted to assimilate the world in its stupendous variety—for himself, for his poems, for his country—and bring it home and make America safe for somebody like Allen Ginsberg. He wanted America to understand why the Allen Ginsberg decked out like Krishna for a couple of hours of chanting and the Allen Ginsberg dressed up in cummerbund and tuxedo for an uptown opening and the Allen Ginsberg wrapped in beads but otherwise naked for a tantric night in Marin County were the same person, and not some fatally divided psyche destined for another round with the doctors at Rockland State. He wanted America to embrace its own variety, which was after all the source of the rhythms and idioms and digressions of the language he chose as an American poet.

I saw Allen very little over the next several years. He was touring a lot then—sometimes to read his poetry, sometimes (in a kind of Bob Dylan–Allen Ginsberg road show) to chant the Blake poems he had set to Eastern music—and I was mainly in Europe, reporting. He showed up though, for the important moments. He had come to Providence once to talk up the graduate student I was going to marry to my mother ("He's cute, Mrs. Kramer," Allen kept saying. "Maybe I'll take him.") And when I had a daughter, he arrived one night for dinner to chant his blessing—to "lay a good mantra on the baby," is the way he put it—and to make sure I remembered the moudra he had taught me in San Francisco, the one for chasing demons away. But after that I saw him mainly when he came to Paris to give a reading or to see his French publishers, Christian and Dominique Bourgois, who had been my own publishers, and were our mutual friends. They always had a party, and Allen loved parties. He loved putting on his suit and being soft-spoken and agreeable and attentive. He loved to *épater la bourgeoisie* by being just like them, and actually he felt quite tender toward what he called "groovy rich ladies." I was never surprise to pick up the *Herald* in Paris and read, say, about Allen Ginsberg and Francesco Clemente arriving together at some fancy party, or about Allen Ginsberg joining a PEN benefit committee with Gayfred Steinberg, because Allen did not discriminate when it came to sharing spiritual information.

Not so long ago, my husband came home from the Graduate Center at the City University of New York, where he teaches, to say that he had just run into Allen in another incarnation: Allen was now a Distinguished Professor of Poetry, and he remarked to my husband in passing that the two of them appeared to be the only professors in the building wearing ties. A few weeks later, we joined Allen at a memorial service for a friend named Ahmed Jacoubi—a Moroccan painter whom Allen had known in Tangiers in the late fififties and early sixties and had introduced to us when we were going there, ten years later. In spirit, Ahmed was as close to Allen as anyone I had ever known, despite the fact that for most of his life he was illiterate. Francis Bacon had taught him to paint; Bill Burroughs and Paul Bowles taught him to make stories; but it was Allen who understood the poet in Ahmed and saw in him a kindred spirit. When Ahmed died, he was living in a loft in Ellen Stewart's Café La Mama annex, and Ellen, who considered herself Ahmed's sister, had arranged the evening so that his friends from both countries—poets and dancers and playwrights and musicians—could invoke their own version of Ahmed's world. Allen read a poem and played his harmonium and chanted, and for a moment he was the Allen I used to know, and not the Allen I had been getting used to—the Allen who was often ill and putting his life in order; the Allen who could talk your ear off about what his biographers were doing, and what his archivists were doing, and what the people collecting his letters were doing; the Allen who was interested in posterity and seemed, sometimes, to be collecting his life instead of living it. In a way, that night at La Mama marked the beginning of the end of a better time. Everybody there felt it, though nobody talked about it—and certainly not Allen. But the last time I saw him—it was six weeks before he died, and we were having dinner together at the artists Alain and Ariane Kirili's loft—Allen spent the evening asking questions. He wanted to know about everybody's life, everybody's work, everybody's children; he wanted to know who was happy and who was miserable or disappointed, and why, and what he could do about it. I said to my husband later that Allen seemed "different" — as if he were going on a trip and collecting *our* lives, the lives of the people who in one way or another had touched his own, to carry with him in his head. People close to Allen say that he didn't know he had cancer until a week before he died, but I think that night he was getting ready to say goodbye.

Allen changed a world, and even if that world has turned out to be much smaller than most of us hoped it was, or could be, back in the days when a boy on the run presented me with Allen's phone number the change was indelible. Allen was indelible. He was enormous.

—JANE KRAMER, June 1997

ALLENGINSBERG
INAMERICA

PART I

"You're such an experimenter, Allen."
—Louis Ginsberg to his son Allen,
Paterson, New Jersey, March 18, 1967

Chapter 1

In January of 1967, on the night before the first evangelical picnic to be called a "Gathering of the Tribes for a Human Be-In," Allen Ginsberg, the poet, took off his shoes and sat down cross-legged on the living-room floor of an apartment in the Haight-Ashbury to preside over what was very likely the oddest planning-committee meeting in San Francisco's crazy and indulgent history. There were eight people in the room with Ginsberg. It was their last chance to arrive at some sort of schedule for the next day's program of poetry readings, sacred Sanskrit chanting, psychedelic rock concerts, and communal love, and they worked hard together, smoothly, for about an hour. Then, when they were down to the last item on the agenda—was the LSD enthusiast Timothy Leary, who was coming to the Be-In all the way from New York, to be considered a poet and therefore allotted seven minutes on the bandstand, or was he, in fact, a bona-fide prophet and therefore entitled to as much as a full half hour?—the committee members found that they could not agree. Philosophically boggled by the fine line between poetry and prophecy, they took a break, at Ginsberg's suggestion, to think things over and wait for guidance. Gary Snyder, a red-bearded Zen monk from the state of Washington who was a poet himself, immediately stripped for meditation down to the earring in his left ear and went to work displacing his rib cage with violent yogic machinations. Near him, a tubby Hasidic book reviewer named Leland Meyerzove started bouncing up and down with his eyes shut tight and was soon transported, wailing softly in tongues. Lenore Kandel, a local love priestess, began belly-dancing in front of an attentive, tweedy English professor from Berkeley, who sucked contemplatively on his pipe, and the poet and playwright Michael McClure, who lived in the apartment, picked up his autoharp from a coffee table and, accompanying himself, cherubically crooned a song that he had just composed called "Come on, God, Buy Me a Mercedes-Benz." The official master of ceremonies for the Be-In, a neighborhood guru with the *nom de psychedélie* of Buddha, wandered around the room in a radiant array of pink, orange, green, and purple silks and velvets, kissing everybody until he was faint from affection and sank down onto the floor next to a pretty young photographer, who was stretched out on her back, taking pictures of the ceiling. The last committee member was Freewheelin' Frank, the secretary of the San Francisco Hell's Angels and the commandant of a Be-In honor guard of motorcycle outlaws who were going to protect the celebrants and their electronic paraphernalia from saboteurs. Freewheelin', who had been leaning against a wall, nodding noncommittally from time to time, took stock of the opportunities for spiritual refreshment at hand, shrugged, and began pacing Mr. Meyerzove's bounces on a tambourine that was fastened to one of the cartridge rings on his leather belt.

Ginsberg himself—forty years old, getting bald and a little myopic—stayed in the middle of the floor, his glasses on and his shoes off, staring at a pair of unmatched socks. He made a comfortable, avuncular presence—a rumpled, friendly-looking man with a nice toothy face, big brown owl eyes behind the horn-rimmed glasses, and a weary, rather affecting slouch. Without his beads and the bushy tangle of a full beard, droopy mustache, and long black ringlets, hanging like a thatch corona from his bald spot, that has become as emblematic as the Beatles' bangs and Albert Einstein's mop of wild white hair, Ginsberg might have passed for the market researcher he once was, in the fifties, for a few years. Tonight he was dressed in chinos, a worn white button-down shirt, and an old striped Shetland sweater. He had put on two necklaces for the meeting—a string of blue Hopi stones and some Yoruba beads, from Cuba, in the seven colors of the seven Yoruba gods—and a metal Mexican Indian god's eye on a piece of rope, and he was wearing a Tibetan oracle's ring on the forefinger of his right hand. On the floor in front of him were two brass finger cymbals from Times Square, and a purple woolen shopping bag from Greece. The bag contained an address book, an appointment pad, one of the School Time composition books in which he likes to jot down thoughts, and a tattered copy of *Prajna Paramita Sutra*, a sacred Buddhist text concerning the ultimate nature of the universe.

"Man, I'd just as soon no one says a word tomorrow," Buddha was saying to Ginsberg, half an hour later, when the thinking was over and the committee had formed a new circle on the floor. "Just beautiful silence. Just everybody sitting around smiling and digging everybody else."

"What we really should have is a sunset celebration on the beach," Ginsberg said.

"Yeah, naked," Snyder said, stepping back into his pants. "That would spook the city of San Francisco."

Ginsberg banged his cymbals. "And maybe, at the end, a groovy naked swim-in," Ginsberg said.

"Tim Leary's a professor—he's not going to want to smile and walk off, *or* swim," Meyerzove broke in, panting a little as he pushed back a peaked astrakhan hat that had slipped down over his forehead during his trance.

"Well, how much time *do* we allow Leary?" Ginsberg asked, laughing. "I say he gets the same time as the poets."

"Is Leary a prima donna?" the girl on her back, Beth Bagby, asked.

"Man, I don't think so—after all, he's taken acid," Buddha replied.

"Leary just needs a little of the responsibility taken off him," Ginsberg said firmly. "Seven minutes, and anyway, if he gets uptight and starts to preach, Lenore can always belly-dance."

Seven minutes were set aside for Leary's speech, and Ginsberg, who had been eying his cymbals, announced that now, if no one minded, he was going to chant. Looking extremely happy, Ginsberg closed his eyes. He rocked for a while to the high, clattering counterpoint of the cymbals, and then he began a mantra to Siva, the Hindu god of destruction, preservation, and *cannabis*. The words of the mantra were "*Hari om namo Sivaye*," and he chanted them slowly at first, in a kind of low, plaintive wail. His voice was deep, sweet, and full of throbs and melodies ("More like a rabbi's than a swami's," Meyerzove whispered to McClure), and soon most of his friends were up and dancing around him. Miss Kandel began to whirl, her arms kneading the air and her stomach rippling to the mantra sounds. Meyerzove shook, groaning ecstatically. Snyder bounded around, samurai-like. Buddha hopped, waving a nursery rattle. And Freewheelin' swayed, jangling his tambourine. Ginsberg chanted faster and faster, until he was sobbing, singing, and laughing at the same time. His head pitched forward with each beat of the cymbals. He seemed on the edge of consciousness, and then, for an instant, he seemed beyond consciousness and part of the strange, hypnotic rhythm of the chant. Suddenly, he was exhausted. He slumped forward with a shudder. One by one the others dropped down onto the floor.

"Wow!" Freewheelin' Frank said.

"We should be doing this tomorrow, in the park, with like five hundred thousand people," Ginsberg said. His eyes were shining.

"Yeah, but for a minute there we were really on our way to the delicatessen," Buddha cried, shaking his head.

Ginsberg jumped up and started laughing. "Hey, I'm hungry," he said. "Who wants to hit the doughnut shop?"

Chapter 2

In a country that has never been very comfortable in the presence of poetic heroes and prophetic poets, Ginsberg is a hero, a prophet, and the man who was largely responsible for the love-happy condition of so many children. He has been revered by thousands of heady, flower-wielding boys and girls as a combination guru and paterfamilias, and by a generation of students—who consider him a natural ally, if for no other reason than that he terrifies their parents with his elaborate and passionate friendliness—as a kind of ultimate faculty adviser. Flower power began in the fall of 1965, when he presented a rally of beleaguered and embittered Berkeley peace marchers with a set of instructions for turning political demonstrations into "exemplary spectacle . . . OUTSIDE the war psychology" which went: "Masses of flowers —a visual spectacle—especially concentrated in the front lines, can be used to set up barricades, to present to Hell's Angels, police, politicians, and press and spectators, whenever needed, or at parade's end . . ." Later, preaching and colonizing a brave new never-never world of bearded, beaded, marijuana-smoking, mantra-chanting euphoria, Ginsberg set the style for the Be-Ins, Love-Ins, Kiss-Ins, Chant-Ins, sacred orgies, and demon-dispelling circumambulations of local draft boards, all of which began with the San Francisco Gathering of the Tribes.

By now, rites like the Gathering and the first epidemic of hippie celebrations have begun to drop back into history. The Haight-Ashbury has outlived its short, exemplary season, and seems to have deteriorated into a bizarre and shadowy nighttown, feeding on some of hippie culture's more grotesque innovations, but the Haight has been replaced as a Utopia by hundreds of thriving hippie enclaves in cities, towns, and campuses across the country. An estimated two hundred thousand children have already left home to try anything from a weekend to a life of sackcloth and marijuana ashes, and from all reports, a few million others have spent a good deal of time wistfully thinking about following them. Over the past few years, while stern city councilmen were busy debating hippie-curbing legislation (in Dallas, where hippies were barred from the downtown business section of the city by an ordinance in the summer of 1967, one impeccably bearded young pediatrician threatened a lawsuit against the municipality when policemen began rerouting his car as he hurried back and forth across town on his house calls), the love people held their ground and, in fact, took over the landscape. They began calling press conferences to announce their metaphysical conclusions, and the media, in reply, took to carrying hippie news items as a matter of national concern. Nearly every national magazine ran off a hippie issue, complete with on-the-spot coverage of the most alarming sort of LSD hallucinatings, and, invariably, an earnest, thoughtful "I Was a Hippie for Two Weeks" essay by one of its younger reporters. The dreary San Francisco press boomed on fillers from the Haight-Ashbury, and the minutiae of life in the East Village

were suddenly being recorded on an almost daily basis in the
New York Times. The television networks, for their part, caught
up by dispatching camera crews to neo-Buddhist festivals and to
teenage "seed power" collectives where crops were tended on advice from the Ouija and the *I Ching.* The hippies, who were al-
ternately worshiped, wooed, and patented, soon became too fash-
ionable to be altogether apocalyptic. By the time a group of
fledgling hippie economists had torn up all their money and
floated it down from the visitors' gallery onto the floor of the New
York Stock Exchange, chanting "Make Love Not Profits" and
ringing bells, several of upper Fifth Avenue's specialty shops were
showing their first psychedelic collections and at least one brokerage house in San Francisco was offering the auxiliary services of a
securities astrologer. Underwear was out and bare feet were *de
rigueur,* according to the women's magazines, which scoured the
underground for signs of chic, and the barber business was trailing far behind the national growth rate, according to the International *Herald Tribune's* annual recap of the 1967 financial
year. Yoga replaced the Canadian Air Force exercises as the latest
antidote to overeating; the Jefferson Airplane was being piped
into office elevators, Greyhound waiting rooms, and Chinese restaurants; corporation couples started taking off their clothes at
parties and painting each other to resemble Day-Glo fantasy
Apache; and a cheerful living-room poster of Ginsberg, whose
name was once synonymous with the word "beat" in all its per-
mutations, became tantamount to a full-blown instant hippie
ambiance.

Ten years, a religious revival, a cold war, a hot war, and lysergic
acid diethylamide, or LSD, separated the beat scene from the
first hippie season. The beats had been, originally, a literary event
—a scattered pack of writers who had broken through, in print
and in person, what Ginsberg once called "the syndrome of shutdown." Almost all of them were born during the Depression,
and they came of age during the Second World War to take up
their pens under the long shadow of McCarthyism and the grim

prosperity that had supported it. Somebody once described them as Hugh Selwyn Mauberleys in sweatshirts. Their holy men were all the pariahs of American life, and they practiced, in print, a meter and a diction drawn from their own extravagant and often desperate experiences. In person, they practiced a sort of sociological hit-and-run, rattling people who were too close to the shutdown and too new to the riches to listen to them. As it turned out, the best thing about the beat credo was the writers who invented it. Its disciples were conspicuous mainly for the thoroughness of their rejections, and they were eventually left behind when the beat literati moved on to explore new ground. Ginsberg spent most of the early sixties traveling around the world, and came home to a generation of postwar babies, who were ready to shed the stigma of real or imagined complicity in the spiritual gap. The coincidence of Ginsberg's homecoming, the Beatles' inauguration of a new sound-sensibility, and Timothy Leary's LSD crusade marked the beginnings of a mystique for them. Someone has called these little hippies champions of the pretty. Their style was somewhat limited by an aesthetic based largely upon the forms of the East as interpreted by novelties manufacturers and appraised, through crystal beads, under the influence of hallucinogens, but they worshiped good intentions, and this in itself was something of a religious leap. (It is difficult to imagine Jack Kerouac arriving at the Stock Exchange with flowers in his hair.) *Their* holy men were holy men, and they invited everybody to join them in a loving universe of family sacraments, group trips, and total rapport. Ginsberg himself was too political to settle down with the hippies for very long. Given the priorities as he saw them, he was happy enough to leave the details of a loving universe to his friends, while he went back to work preserving the universe at hand. That July, he flew to London for a long symposium, called the "Dialectics of Liberation," with Ronald Lang, Paul Goodman, Gregory Bateson, Stokely Carmichael, and Herbert Marcuse, and then, in the fall, he took a room in a *pensione* in Venice, next door to Ezra Pound, to start to put together three new books of journals and poems. From Europe, he plotted what was very likely the first American exorcism ritual since the Navaho Enemy Way, whipped up a fine Pentagon mantra as an accompaniment, and by other appropriate means, directed in absentia the mass circumambulation of the Defense Department by several thousand demonstrators on October 21 that year. The anniversary of the San Francisco Gathering of the Tribes for a Human Be-In found him in court in New York, accused of having blocked the entrance to the Whitehall Street Induction Center during End the Draft Week. (He pleaded guilty to a misdemeanor and was given an unconditional discharge. It was his first conviction, and his neighbors, who wanted him to run for President, were very unhappy about this.) A few weeks later, he turned up at a rally at Town Hall, protesting the indictment of Dr. Benjamin Spock. He spent the rest of January digging up information on the sins of the American military-industrial complex, and then in February, armed with statistics, he left for a tour of some thirty or forty colleges. In March he was in Washington, talking to Robert Kennedy about the war in Vietnam, and when the Democrats met in Chicago, he was there with his bells on, ready for a "mass manifestation of gaiety" with a few hundred thousand of his friends.

Out in the world, Ginsberg has proved to be so irreproachably immune to the rewards held out to tractable, commercial, or socially decorative bohemians that over the past few years he has become something of a symbol of the profound and often comic incompatibilities between the values of the Establishment and the values of an amalgamated hippie-pacifist-activist-visionary-orgiastic-anarchist-orientalist-psychedelic underground whose various causes and commitments he always managed to espouse. He has been the subject of more argument between the generations than any American poet since Whitman, whom he admires, and his impact has perhaps been even stronger than Whitman's, because whether people are enthusiastic about Ginsberg or enraged by him—"the unjust equation of *my* long hair with *their* nightmare visions of some monster beatnik," Ginsberg says—people who know or know *of* Ginsberg seem to put a great deal of energy into reacting to him. Much of Ginsberg's mail, which is voluminous, comes from strangers: "Dear Allen, This letter was written due to a line where you stated 'Communicate with me.' Do you realize that you would not be you if not for me? Please acknowledge my presence," and "Dear Mr. Ginsberg, Occasional escape from reality is good, but it seems to me that you are too real . . . and your 'ultra' reality in which you blot out the unreal shows you're not really where it's at and probably just an exhibitionist." Some people need advice: "Dear Allen, How do I become a poet? Could you just tell me *something* about it?" and "Dear Allen, I am very sad and want to ask you whether or not you believe that an innate capacity for opening the mind and loosening the heart exists in all, however angry, afraid, submerged they may be?" and "Dear Allen, I am a student at Loyola College in Baltimore and it was in this academically sterile institution that I first came into contact with your work through and under the guidance of the only fertile mind on campus. Being a student with many interests in the field of literature, and at the same time, being a *person*, I am searching for reconciliation through art and the self . . . I am twenty years old and do not expect magical solutions. Merely insight, and a new view. Would you correspond with me?" Others want information: "Dear Allen Ginsberg, I plan on heading toward northern India and Nepal and on to Japan, if necessary, in search of a guru. I know that to begin with there are not that many left to be found, but I was wondering what my chances would be of finding one that spoke English. If you knew of any specific areas where I might locate one, or better yet, if you happen to know of certain individuals who might instruct me on my search for the realization of the truth, I would appreciate it

very much if you would let me know . . ." and "Dear Mr.
Ginsberg, In my English course we are required to write ten
short papers on various topics. You are my first topic . . ." In one
day's batch of mail, Ginsberg received requests for a character
reference and guarantee of financial support from a Japanese
poet who wanted a permanent visa with which to enter the
country; for a piece of his beard (which he immediately clipped
and mailed) for the annual fund-raising sale of a high-school
literary club in Bakersfield, California; for a manuscript (which he
sent) for auction at a benefit in London for the relief of South
African political prisoners; for another manuscript (which he
also sent) for auction at a benefit in France for a new committee to end the Vietnam war; and for a love potion of his
own choosing—"If you are whimsical or have time, send something to the boy I love. He has had acid already. I wish it worked,"
—which he did nothing about. He also had a note from an Albuquerque jail. It went: "Mr. Ginsberg, I am also a poet . . . I
was arrested in Albuquerque, New Mexico, late last year for possession of the herb; three dollars' worth. I am now awaiting trial.
My sentence is to be from two to ten years. May I, Mr. Ginsberg,
with your permission, read your statement on marijuana from the
Atlantic Monthly at my trial? . . . I saw you once from afar and
said, 'Hello, Mr. Soul.' "

Ginsberg's friends write to let him know *where* they are—
"Dear Allen, Another day in the bug house!" and "I am on
my way to India and the India beyond India but I will see you
before and there, of course. You were right. Siva really dances!"
—and to keep him up to date on what is happening there: "Dear
Allen, Things really seem to be in a state of chaos here in London. The news—first, twelve policemen visited the bookstore on
Thursday last week. They went at once downstairs to the paper
and began searching all the ashtrays and rubbish bins, presumably
for roaches and dog ends containing 'suspicious substances.' They
seized *all* back issues of the *International Times* (about 10,000
copies), including all the reference copies, they didn't leave us

one . . . and from the shop they seized all the copies we had of: *Naked Lunch, I, Jan Cremer, Memoirs of a Shy Pornographer,* by Patchen, *The Sonnets* by Ted Berrigan . . ." and, "Hello, Allen, The students at the London School of Economics are 'doing a Berkeley.' They have been holding sit-downs, fasts, marches with flowers, etc., and recently declared a formation of an 'open university' within the school . . . The students are really causing a stir, getting front-page coverage in all the newspapers, TV, etc . . . But the great thing is that everyone— poets, pop stars, students, intellectuals, kids—is moving together into a united force in reaction to the official heavy hand."

Ginsberg answers all his letters. He puts them first into a big worn Manila envelope with "unanswered" scribbled over an old address. Then they go into a second worn Manila envelope— —this one marked "answered"—which in turn is stuffed into one of the innumerable bulging cartons labeled "letters" that are stacked in a vaguely chronological order on his bedroom floor. Important communiqués, such as letters about drug laws and obscenity trials, get clipped, underlined, and filed away in an appropriate folder in the cross-referenced file cabinet in Ginsberg's dining room.

One of his friends has called Ginsberg the central casting office of the underground. He enters the name, address, and phone number of anyone he meets who plays, or is apt to play, a part in what he thinks of as the new order—or has information that might be useful to it—in the address book that he always carries in his purple bag, and he goes to considerable trouble putting people he likes in touch with each other and with sympathetic and influential Establishment characters who might be helpful to them. In this way, Ginsberg has managed to create a network of the like-minded around the world. Any one of his friends who goes to a city that Ginsberg has ever visited knows in advance where to stay, whom to see, and what local statutes to avoid breaking, not to mention who the local shamen are, what politicians are friendly, who has bail money, who sells pot, the temperament of the chief of police, the sympathies of the editors of all the newspapers, the phone numbers of the local activists, and where the best sex and the best conversation can be found. Ginsberg's passion for an entirely *comunicado* underground has made him the most practically effective drop-out around. He has contacts in Washington and most of the big city halls, as well as in law firms, Civil Liberties Union offices, and universities scattered across the country. And, with most of the information that he needs at his fingertips, Ginsberg can accomplish with a phone call what many of his friends would take months to muddle through. When Robert Kennedy was alive, Ginsberg would direct an East Village neighbor with a problem to the Senator's office—"Call. They owe me a favor"—and now, with the aplomb of a bank president, he will ring up the mayor of San Francisco for a hippie-in-distress or recommend a lawyer with a complete run-down of pertinent cases undertaken and a conclusive "Use him . . . he's good . . . he turns on." Ginsberg's friend Gregory Corso, the poet, once complained that Ginsberg was operating like a Jewish businessman, but all of his friends agree that as an operator Ginsberg is invaluable. Few of them have either Ginsberg's talent for coping with the tangly protocols and bewildering façades of the square world *or* his tolerance and affection for its unregenerate inhabitants. He likes most people, and consequently he does not share the compulsion of many of his companions to dismiss them, avoid them, or put them down. Ginsberg tries his best to be soothing rather than startling. He will scold a friend for frightening a fellow-being on the other side of the Establishment fence by "coming on like some spooky superexclusive angry beatnik egomaniac madman," and he works hard to assure everybody that nothing human, even Ginsberg, is really terribly alarming.

"I hope that whatever prejudgment you may have of me or my bearded image you can suspend so that we can talk together as fellow-beings in the same room of NOW, trying to come to some harmony and peacefulness between us" was the way he introduced himself to Senators Quentin Burdick, Jacob Javits, and Edward Kennedy at a special Judiciary Subcommittee hearing on narcotics legislation in the spring of 1966. "I am a little frightened to present myself—the fear of your rejection of me, the fear of not being tranquil enough to reassure you that we can talk together, make sense, and perhaps even *like* each other, enough to want not to offend, or speak in a way which is abrupt or hard to understand." Senator Javits, who was a little jittery at being in a room of NOW with Ginsberg, interrupted the poet to tell him not to worry so much about his bearded image, but Ginsberg went along calmly, talking to the senators about his peyote visions, about learning to like women better under the good influence of ayahuasca, and about praying for Lyndon Johnson's "tranquil health" after taking LSD in a cliff cove at Big Sur, on the day of the President's gall-bladder operation. He told the senators to think of LSD as a "useful educational tool" and —this was long before any statistics that could be considered reliable had been compiled on the pros and cons of LSD—to consider the possibility that the terror preceding most of the acid breakdowns that had been reported was an effect not of the drug itself, but of threatening laws and unfriendly social circumstances. Then he said that to *really* discourage the use of LSD, the senators should supply the kind of society in which "nobody will need it to break through to common sympathy." The senators were no more unnerved by this piece of advice than, on the other hand, Timothy Leary was one night when Ginsberg told *him* that in a "groovy" society drugs like LSD would be irrelevant. Leary had just invited Ginsberg to join him on an "LSD march around the world." Ginsberg replied that, in his opinion, it would be far more sensible for everybody to stay home and help the government figure out how to stop the war. "All I'm trying to do, really," Ginsberg said later, "is get the people who smoke pot and take acid talking to the people who don't and clear up some of the paranoia around."

The people "who don't" are apt to have learned about Ginsberg's mission—Senator Burdick introduced Ginsberg to his colleagues as the Pied Piper of the drug movement—from newspaper pictures of the poet chanting "*Hare Krishna*" at one of Leary's sellout psychedelic celebrations or marching across Sheridan Square with a big grin on his face and a homemade sign saying POT IS FUN! pinned to his overcoat. Actually, Ginsberg has put in years researching the ins and outs of the marijuana laws and compiling the historical, scientific, and religious arguments against them. Marijuana, known in its various incarnations as hemp, hashish, ganga, kef and *Cannibis sativa*, is evidently smoked, chewed, baked into cakes or brewed into tea and enjoyed as a daily pick-me-up in a good part of the Hindu, Islamic, African, and Latin-American world, and as often as not by people who regard the ingestion of alcohol as tantamount to venial sin; and the official panic about the herb in the United States has therefore always been something of a mystery to travelers like Ginsberg, who has shared it by the pipeful with Arab Sufi and sipped it in milk with the professors in Indian faculty clubs. It was legal in this country, in fact, until a one-time Prohibition officer by the name of Harry Anslinger took over the newly created Federal Bureau of Narcotics, shortly before Repeal. Apparently, no one in the Bureau had thought much about marijuana one way or another until the commissioner discovered "the marijuana menace"—I told the story of this evil weed of the fields and riverbeds and roadsides . . . The public was alerted!" Anslinger wrote many years later in a professional autobiography of sorts, which Ginsberg likes to keep on his bookshelf next to one of his favorite tantric reference volumes, *Sexual Practices in Ancient China*—and this has prompted Ginsberg to what he calls a scholarly marijuana theory, involving Parkinson's Law that a bureaucrat will always attempt to find work for himself. Anslinger steered through a curiously unquestioning Congress the country's first marijuana-control bill, the Marijuana Tax Act of 1937, and within a few years he managed to convert the Bureau from a tiny Treasury Department offshoot, concerned with the collection of opiate taxes, into a massive watchdog operation with a staff of agents and near autonomy within the government. Under Anslinger, and more recently under Harry Giordano, the new commissioner, the Bureau, which is empowered to prefer federal "possession" charges carrying high mandatory minimum sentences, has gotten embroiled in a running war of wits with Ginsberg and his friends. The war involves matchpoint propaganda—once, in 1961, Ginsberg attacked the Bureau on a Saturday-night television panel show, and the Bureau demanded, and received, equal time—and a good deal of tactical one-upmanship. The Bureau, which used to train agents as beatniks, now has a crack corps of hippies and "students" circulating in the universities and through the underground. (Ginsberg discovered an agent—or thought he had—in the Haight-Ashbury one winter. The suspected narc, as Bureau policemen were referred to at the moment, was a chummy and extravagantly hip young man who dressed in an assortment of hippie-beat-Hell's-Angel–Berkeley-activist regalia that left no association unturned. He appeared regularly at all the hippie hangouts, but no one ever saw him at the straight places that hippies enjoy, such as restaurants, department stores, supermarkets, and dinner parties in big houses. Encountering Ginsberg, he would barrage the poet with in-references, in-language, and a good deal of uncharitable chatter about "squares," a habit which Ginsberg considered not only ungentlemanly but an almost certain giveaway. And what was apparently most significant, he betrayed none of the suspicion, common to *real* marijuana people, that narcotic agents were around.) Ginsberg, on the other hand, now keeps a volunteer "marijuana secretary" cataloguing the clippings, documents, and correspondence that accumulate in his apartment, and his marijuana file is one of the most complete and accurate private records of its kind. (His favorite among the marijuana articles he has turned out, a long piece for the *Atlantic Monthly* that he called "The Great Marijuana Hoax," was sprinkled with footnotes and citations from such ponderous and unlikely authorities as the 1925 Panama Canal Zone Governor's Committee's report on marijuana and the *Report of the British India Hemp Commission, 1893-1894* and included the charming statistic, "I have spent about as many hours high as I have spent in movie theaters—sometimes three hours a week, sometimes twelve or twenty or more, as at a film festival.") Reporters use the file; so do the students and scholars of the marijuana movement who live around New York. Lawyers preparing marijuana cases refer to Ginsberg's papers, and they are the basis of the poet's own latest marijuana project—the sponsorship and support of a brief to the effect that the existing marijuana statutes violate the legal rights of artists to the necessary materials of their trade. Ginsberg would like to use the brief in Washington, eventually, in a test case in the Supreme Court. It will take some fifty thousand dollars, he expects, to cover costs.

Ginsberg likes to call his own well-known experiments with marijuana and the hallucinogens "pious investigations." He often compares himself, in this respect, to the French Symbolist poets, and, like them, he has kept a faithful record of his investigations in poems and journals written over the years and under a variety of influences, from psilocybin mushrooms to his dentist's laughing gas. The first of these, a journal, covered the day he took peyote for the first time: Ginsberg was in Paterson, New Jersey, at his father's house, and after gagging down the last of the peyote, which is terrible-tasting stuff, he sat down to a phantasmagoric Sunday dinner with a crowd of bickering and unsuspecting relatives. His published letters from Peru to William Burroughs (and from an earlier trip by Burroughs, Burroughs' letters to him) were written under and about yagé, which is an hallucinogenic brew distilled by the local *curanderos* from a vine called *Banisteriopsis caape*. Part II of his poem "Howl" was inspired by a peyote vision that Ginsberg had in San Francisco, staring out of his window one night at the tower of the Sir Francis Drake Hotel and being reminded of Moloch by the tower's grinning, mask-like façade; the elegy to his mother, "Kaddish," was the product of forty-odd hours awake and high on a combination of amphetamines; and the recent "Wales Visitation," which Ginsberg calls his "first great big Wordsworthian nature poem," was written under LSD.

In the course of more eclectic pious investigations, Ginsberg also has meditated toward sartori with a Zen roshi in Kyoto, made fire magic with a North African witch doctor, shared hemp and nakedness with the burning ghat saddhus in Calcutta, explored the spiritual transports of yogic breathing and "chant turn-on" with Swami A. C. Bhaktivedanta, circumambulated sacred Indian mountains in California, burned butter to Siva with a Sanskrit teacher at Columbia, and communed with the Oakland Hell's Angels through a split sacrament of the *Prajna Paramita Sutra* and LSD. Lately, he has been writing poems with titles such as "Consulting *I Ching* Smoking Pot Listening to the Fugs Sing Blake," "Wichita Vortex Sutra," and "The Holy Ghost on the Nod Over the Body of Bliss," and he has been waving good-bye, whenever he goes out, to a little private shrine on a bookshelf above his television set. The shrine consists of his Tibetan oracle's ring, an Islamic amulet, a small bronze laughing Ho Te Buddha, a miniature of Krishna and Radha, a Maltese cross, a zodiac poster, some picture postcards of his favorite Christian martyrs, a package of cigarette papers, and a photograph of his roommate of the past thirteen years, Peter Orlovsky, posing naked as a Jain saint.

One night at the hot springs of the Esalen Institute in Big Sur, Ginsberg, who was looking forward to a panel discussion on religion with Snyder, Bishop James Pike, and Harvey Cox of the Harvard Divinity School, found himself sharing a bathtub with a group of visiting Episcopal ministers and their wives. After a long talk about Christianity, punctuated by emphatic, sulphurous splashings on all sides, one of the ministers asked Ginsberg what exactly his religion was. Ginsberg slid deep into the water and began thinking about this. After a while, he said that he was probably a "Buddhist Jew," with attachments to Krishna, Siva, Allah, Coyote, and the Sacred Heart. Then he said no—he was simply on a sort of pilgrimage, "shopping around." In a minute he corrected himself again, saying that he really thought *all* the gods were "groovy," and so, in fact, he was more of a Buddhist Jewish *pantheist*. Climbing out of the steaming yellow water, he pointed to Orlovsky, who was perched on a railing by the ocean conversing in loud, braying noises with the full moon. "I figure one sacrament's as good as the next one, if it works," Ginsberg said.

Chapter 3

The day of the first Gathering of the Tribes for a Human Be-in was hot and splendidly sunny, and the twenty or so thousand people who came to the Polo Field in San Francisco's Golden Gate Park had been able to Be in their brightest, barest psychedelic costumes, without the dreary camouflage of overcoats and boots. In fact, according to Michael Bowen, a young Haight-Ashbury painter with an inspirational tale of having been saved from an amphetamine habit by a combination of love, Tantrism, and LSD, Mexico had generously exchanged climates with Northern California, at the intercession of Bowen's Mexican guru, in the interests of a thoroughly successful day. (Bowen said later that it had snowed hard in Mexico.) Ginsberg himself had come to the park in a pair of blue rubber bathing thongs, which he had picked up at a Japanese stall on the way over to the park, and a white hospital orderly's uniform which he likes to wear for ceremonial events. Now, seven hours later, with his dress whites muddy, sweaty, and stained by flowers, he was hunting for his new sandals under piles of electronic-rock equipment on a deserted bandstand at the end of the field. It was a calm, pink twilight. People were moving in slow, sleepy coveys toward the road. Ginsberg, who had just led them in silent meditation on the setting sun and in a closing mantra—"*Om Sri Maitreya*"—to the Buddha of the Future, watched them disappear over the crest of a hill that bordered the field. He looked elated, exhausted, and a little sick to his stomach from all the fruit, cookies, candy bars, cigarettes, Cokes, and peanut-butter sandwiches that had been pressed on him by his admirers, and he was covered from head to toe with gifts of beads, bells, amulets, buttons, and one enormous, dazzling, flowered tie.

It had been a beautiful day, Ginsberg told a boy who climbed up onto the bandstand to say good night and to admire the tie, which the poet held out proudly, saying, "Hey, look! Someone laid this groovy tie on me today." He had arrived at the park at eleven, before the crowds, in order to chant some Buddhist *dharanis*, or short-form prayers, for removing whatever disasters might be hovering in the vicinity and to circumambulate the field —a purification ritual that he had learned from the Hindus, who always circumambulate *their* fields before a *mela*, which is a similarly gala Indian gathering of seekers and holy men. The Hell's Angels had pulled up on their Harley-Davidsons a little while later, as promised, to guard the generators and trunk lines for the rock groups who were going to play, and although Freewheelin' had fallen off a sound truck onto a ketchup bottle and cut his face in several places, he had been the only casualty of the day. Someone *had* slashed one of the feed lines to a sound truck belonging to the Grateful Dead, a rock band which took its name from the passage "In the land of the dark the ship of the sun is driven by the grateful dead," in the Egyptian Book of the Dead, but it had been repaired quickly, and one of the Dead musicians, who wanted to make a citizen's arrest on a heckler "for destroying my sanity," had been quietly persuaded that the destruction of sanity was a Constitutional prerogative. Timothy Leary and Jerry Rubin, the Berkeley activist—Rubin had been bailed out of jail that morning especially for the Be-In—both had made short, loving speeches, to the great relief of the planning committee. (Leary, actually, had spent most of the day on the bandstand playing pat-a-cake with a steady succession of stray children.) A young man in a black mask had floated down from the sky, attached to a paisley parachute, and landed in the middle of the field, frightening a few of the picnickers but giving rise to considerable speculation among the others as to whether the Buddha of the Future had not, in fact, appeared at last. A sulphur bomb, planted by a nonbeliever, had exploded under the bandstand at three in the afternoon, but by that time the celebrants in the immediate area had been so euphoric that they took it for a new brand of incense and applauded enthusiastically. Roshi Shunryu Suzuki, the master of the Soto Zen Center in San Francisco, had arrived unexpectedly shortly after the bomb went off, carrying a wreath of flowers and followed by a human chain of brown-robed disciples, and *he* had smiled his blessing on the vast, frolicking manifestation of illuminated consciousness. The costumes had been beautiful. There had been Colonial petticoats, buckskins and war paint, Arabian desert robes, paisley body stockings on the girls and paisley diapers on the babies, Hopi tops and Hindu bottoms, mistletoe cod flaps, bedspreads, capes, togas, and ancestral velvets. Roughly one-fortieth of the population of greater San Francisco had spent the afternoon in the park together, and the word had been sounded by the poets: "Peace in your heart dear/ Peace in the park here" (Ginsberg); "Let it go, whatever you do is beautiful" (Kandel); and "This is really it, and it is all perfect" (McClure).

Looking at the boy on the bandstand, Ginsberg grinned. The boy was wearing a suit of armor which he had draped with rosebuds, daisies, and daffodils. He was a peace warrior, he said. "I guess you can tell by the way I'm dressed," he added. "I kind of dig freedom."

"I wish I had a camera," Ginsberg said. Then he jumped off the bandstand and ran up the hill to catch his friends.

Ginsberg was due at Bowen's place on Haight Street for a macrobiotic supper and some chanting, and a half hour later he was standing in front of one of the fancy, battered Victorian buildings that lined the street and managed to give it a somewhat less belligerently shabby face than the hippie enclaves in Chicago and New York. He was with a girl called Maretta, a gaunt, shy sibyl of twenty-four who had been traveling with Ginsberg since her return that fall from India, where she had spent two years in relentless pursuit of her *sadhana*, or true path. Maretta had heard about India from a meditative fellow passenger on a Greyhound bus from Boston to New York, which happened to get stuck in the snow for several hours near New Rochelle, and she had hitchhiked there, through Europe and on across Turkey, Persia, and Afghanistan. In the course of a job she found there teaching English to nine-year-old incarnate lamas at a Himalayan summer school, she had formally converted to Tibetan Buddhism, which was the favorite Buddhism of all the visionary people then. At the moment, Maretta was talking to Ginsberg about her *sadhana*, which she believed to be hashish this time around in her cycle of rebirth. They had been watching the street for Peter Orlovsky, and for Peter's older brother, Julius, both of whom they had lost track of at some point during the afternoon. Peter Orlovsky, an admittedly loony lyric poet of manic compassions, was in the habit of wandering off with a rag and a big bottle of Lysol to scrub down cars, stoops, windows and sidewalks, in line with his own *sadhana*, which was keeping the universe clean. His brother also had a habit of disappearing. Julius had once spent twelve years in a hospital, completely silent, and even now, with Ginsberg and

Orlovsky looking after him, he rarely said a word. Ginsberg told Maretta that he suspected Julius of having taken off at the Be-In to have a secret talk.

Ginsberg and Maretta waited on the sidewalk for five more minutes, leaving messages for the Orlovskys with an assortment of hippie pedestrians, and then they climbed the flight of stairs to Bowen's apartment, where the post-celebration celebration was already under way. Bowen greeted them at the door—a big, gangly young man, with a mop of fuzzy brown hair, rosy cheeks, and a boyish gap between his two front teeth. He had thrown off his dress shirt—an elaborate purple jerkin—at one point during the Be-In, but he still wore several strands of beads and a pair of expensive-looking brown suede pants. Maretta admired them, and Bowen complimented *her* on her own costume—Maretta had on flowing hounds'-tooth culottes, red on one leg and green on the other, an orange middy blouse, and a red fringed head shawl, and she was trailing a length of gauzy purple sari cloth. Then he announced that, according to the calculations of Gavin Arthur, Chester Arthur's grandson and a local clairvoyant, the population of the earth at that particular moment in time was equivalent to the total of all the dead in human history.

"That means we're all back, we're all together," Bowen said.

"Fucking beautiful," Maretta murmured.

"Groovy," Ginsberg said. "Are we too late for dinner?"

Bowen pointed down the hall to a brightly lit kitchen, where a young woman in a long green corduroy skirt was standing over a stove, dishing out brown rice to a line of wan and softly chanting hippie girls. The young woman was called Lavinia. She had already abandoned her last name, which she did not feel expressed the "real" her, when she first left home for San Francisco, and now, at twenty-one, Lavinia was a veteran hippie householder. She had settled down with Bowen in the fall, after several months of purifying meditation alone in a tent at Big Sur, and her experience in the woods as a hunter-gatherer-meditator had made her a heroine to the newer arrivals in the Haight-Ashbury, who regarded her retreat as something of an ultimate gesture. Whereas Bowen was admired for the aphorisms of hippie life which he regularly loosed on visiting reporters from the news weeklies—"The psychedelic baby eats the cybernetic monster in San Francisco" and "We are building an electric Tibet in California" were two of his favorites—Lavinia was famous locally as an expert on non-poisonous berries, outdoor mantra chanting, latrine digging, and all-weather dressmaking. Ginsberg had known her since the fall of 1966, when they had gone on a five-week camping and climbing trip with Snyder to the Northern Cascades, and he greeted her warmly, helping himself to a slice of damp, leaden, homemade wheat-germ bread that was lying on the kitchen table. Then he introduced her to Maretta, who said, "Got any hash, man?"

"My yoga at the moment is cooking," Lavinia answered dryly. "Feeding everybody with good natural breads and oats and corn. Seeing that the people here get wholesome, vegetarian food."

"My yoga is giving up smoking—that is, until this week it was," Ginsberg said, laughing. He reached into his jacket pocket for a Pall Mall. "In New York I met this really groovy swami named Satchidananda. At a party Christmas Eve, I think it was. And I was complaining about smoking too much, and like he said that giving up smoking could be interpreted as a valid form of yoga. Like it involves all the yogic disciplines—control of temper, concentration, devotion, the happy concurrence of body and mind. So like I vowed then and there to stop, and I was doing all right till I hit San Francisco." Ginsberg shrugged, looking ashamed of himself.

Lavinia handed Ginsberg a plateful of steaming rice, and he stayed in the kitchen for a while, eating and gossiping. Then, with Maretta in tow, he wandered down the hall, following the sound of voices, bells, and cymbals and the sharp mingled smells of incense and tobacco, to a small square room that was dimly lit by a set of fat black dripping candles. The room, which was Bowen's meditation room, was hung with the patterned batik bedspreads then in service in psychedelic circles as everything from wallpaper to evening gowns. Mattresses had been laid out side by side around the walls, and in the middle of the room, on a worn oriental rug, there was a low scrolled wooden table with a candelabra, a saucer of burning incense, a tiny bronze Buddha, and a scattering of flowers. The remains of a light-bulb fixture on the ceiling were draped with bells, god's-eyes, and long strands of crystal beads that dipped down almost to the floor and swung, tinkling, whenever anybody touched them. One of Bowen's paintings, an LSD vision of eyes, hearts, broad squiggly lines and strange Coptic-looking configurations, was tacked to one of the bedspreads next to an aquatint of Mary and Jesus at an angel party of some sort, and across the room, taking up most of a wall, was a large and extremely rare Tibetan tanka, or silk scroll painting, of the Maitreya. (Snyder had discovered the scroll in Kyoto, Ginsberg had paid for it, and they had entrusted it to Bowen for use as an altarpiece as soon as the first "indigenous American ashram" opened in the Haight-Ashbury.)

About eighteen people, all in their Be-In costumes, were snuggled into companionable heaps on the thin mattresses in Bowen's meditation room. Some of them were talking or chanting quietly to themselves. The others were staring amiably into space. They were all in the process of sharing a peace pipe, when Ginsberg and Maretta, tripping over a pile of people on the threshold, stumbled in. Maretta headed for a dark corner, where she staked out a few feet of mattress, curled up into a ball of culottes and fringe, and almost instantly fell asleep. Ginsberg located Snyder on a mattress behind the candelabra and sat down next to him. Snyder was wearing clothes—a pair of green corduroy jeans and a green blouse blocked with big mauve leaves and flowers—and waving around a gallon jug of California Bordeaux. Just as Ginsberg reached for the jug, a light went on, and two television men, dragging kliegs and cables, began maneuvering toward him. They said that Bowen had invited them. Ginsberg groaned.

"I don't know why, but this whole day strikes me as absolutely sane and right and beautiful," one of the men said cheerfully, holding a light meter up to Ginsberg's nose. "Mike must have put something in my tea last night."

"What's so *in*sane about a little peace and harmony?" Ginsberg asked him, inching over on the mattress to make room for Maretta, who had been awakened by the light.

Maretta nodded sleepily, "It was fucking beautiful," she said.

"Like *thousands* of people would like to come to the park on a day like today," Ginsberg went on. "So they can relate to each other as—as dharma beings. All sorts of people. Poets, children, even Hell's Angels. People are lonesome. *I'm* lonesome. It's strange to be in a body. So what I'm doing—what we're all doing —on a day like today is saying, 'Touch me, sleep with me, *talk* to me.' "

"People are groovy," Snyder said.

"Zap!" Ginsberg said, and snapped his fingers. "You know how Reagan said, 'Once you've seen one redwood tree you've seen them all . . .' "

"That's an incredible mentality to us," Snyder broke in.

"Actually, I used to be in love with Reagan in the thirties—I used to see all his movies," Ginsberg said, smiling ingenuously. "So Ronald Reagan and I are one. Ronald Reagan, you and I are *one!*"

Bowen, who had just come running into the room with a telephone in his hand, called to Ginsberg that he had Santa Barbara on the line. "In Santa Barbara, they meditated with us for six whole hours while we were at the Be-In," Bowen shouted as he leapt over a mattress, dropped down onto his hands and knees, and began tossing aside pillows until he located an extension socket in the wall.

"You mean to say you have a phone in your meditation room?" Ginsberg said, and burst out laughing.

"Electric Tibet, baby," Bowen said, flipping Ginsberg the receiver. "Say something, will you, Allen?"

"Hello, what's your name?" Ginsberg said, sticking a finger in his free ear. "Bright? Hey, that's a groovy name." Ginsberg turned to Snyder. "His name is Bright. That's nice." And then back to Santa Barbara. "We're just saying that Ronald Reagan should prove his good faith by turning on."

"In the middle of the redwood forest, tell him," Snyder shouted.

Bowen reached for the phone. "It's really far out here, man," Bowen said.

Ginsberg peered at the television man, who was crawling around him with a long microphone cord in his hand.

"Take the phone call," Ginsberg told the television man. "It's like we're bridging the gap between all sorts of people with this —this kind of community festival. I thought it was very Eden-like today, actually. Kind of like Blake's vision of Eden. Music. Babies. People just sort of floating around having a good time and everybody happy and smiling and touching and turning each other on and a lot of groovy chicks all dressed up in their best clothes and—"

"But will it *last?*" the television man said.

Ginsberg shrugged. "How do *I* know if it will last?" he said. "And if it doesn't turn out, who cares?"

"I met a policeman at the park who really dug the consciousness today," a boy in a plaid blanket whispered from across the room. "He told me that he thought today was beautiful."

"Even the Hell's Angels dug the consciousness," Ginsberg added, nodding. "Like they were all turned into big happy benevolent beings."

The television man wanted to know how important LSD was to this new benevolence.

"Come on, there are other yogas besides LSD, you know," Ginsberg said. "Chanting, for one. Sex. Love. Giving up smoking. And running laps—that's also yoga." Ginsberg stopped to pat a baby who had crawled into the meditation room and was reaching for his beard, gurgling curiously.

"Acid just happened to turn up as the product of this particular society, to correct its own excesses," Snyder began.

The television man signaled to his partner, who had moved back to the door and was standing there with a hand-held camera, to start shooting. They worked for a half hour and had just run out of film when Timothy Leary, in a bright red Aran Islands sweater, rushed into the room. Leary was a little out of breath, and so was his Los Angeles lawyer, a man in a pink shirt and a tweed Eisenhower jacket, who ran in after him.

"Out there, on the street," the lawyer, whose name was Seymour Lazar, called to the meditators. "Five paddy wagons! At least five. And they're arresting kids right and left."

"What for *now*?" Ginsberg asked them.

"Nondispersal or something," Leary said. "All I know is that we were taking a walk up Haight Street and heard a group of kids singing outside the Psychedelic Shop, and then suddenly the police arrived, out of nowhere, and started busting everybody."

"Well, they're not busting *us*," Snyder said.

"But they're grabbing hostages, and for a reason," Bowen, who was pulling on his jerkin, said. "Terror's the reason, man."

Most of the people in the room nodded.

"Oh, come on," Ginsberg said, getting up and heading for the stairs. "The police are people. They're just a little paranoid. Something must have scared them. Anyway, I'm going down and have a look around."

Ginsberg left with Leary, Lazar, and a few people from the party. He came back about fifteen minutes later, and he stuck his head into the meditation room to say, "Someone threw a bottle or something," and then went into a huddle with Lazar and Leary on the kitchen table. He told Lazar that the Haight needed to organize and hire a lawyer to handle its troubles with the police.

"You see, if you've got trouble—LSD, marijuana, prostitution —just talk to Seymour," Leary told some boys and girls who had followed the men to the kitchen and were standing, at the door, listening.

"Well, there's nothing we can do tonight," Ginsberg said finally. He was perched on the table, in between several loaves of fresh natural bread.

"Tell me something, Allen," Lazar, who had been watching Ginsberg, said suddenly. "You must have a little money now. You can *afford* things. Tell me why you stay in such funky places."

"How do *you* know?" Ginsberg demanded. "You ever been to one of our funky places?" He began chanting cheerfully at the lawyer.

"And all this chanting," Lazar said. "You're such a *rabbi*."

Ginsberg shrugged. "It's kicks," he said. "*Hare Krishna*, Seymour." Ginsberg hopped off the table and, still chanting, padded barefoot back into the meditation room. Snyder welcomed him with a blast from a conch horn that he had blown to the four winds at the Be-In that afternoon.

The conch was wrapped in blue net and garlanded with wildflowers, and Ginsberg, who said that he thought the horn looked very magical, began to talk to it. "Tell me, O conch, will I have to give up fucking at the fourth level of enlightenment?" Ginsberg held the conch to his ear and waited for an answer.

Everyone giggled but a young man in a turn-of-the-century Merchant Marine dress uniform, who had been staring sullenly at Ginsberg from a mattress across the room. "Here you are, the great Ginsberg, sitting there talking like this was *your* scene," the boy said.

"We had some of this scene going ten years ago," Ginsberg told him. "At least some of us were accomplishing *something* like this then."

"Yeah, but then there were ten years when you had nothing to say to the world," the boy said.

"You're right." Ginsberg nodded agreeably.

The boy glared and added, "Anyway, I didn't mean *this* scene, like here tonight. I meant the *communal* scene."

"But we had a communal thing going too," Ginsberg said, chuckling. "The trouble was that less people wanted to commune."

Snyder spoke up, looking at the boy. "I'd say the big difference between our old scene and now is *this*. We had a friend then— a poet—who killed himself, and he took a lot of shit, magically speaking, with him when he died. We knew we didn't need or want that kind of self-defeating scene any more."

"Anyway, we *did* have a big friendly family scene," Ginsberg said. "It's recorded literary history. Anybody who wants to can look it up." Ginsberg glanced around the room. "Like we even took off our clothes at parties."

"Well, why not now, or on the street, man?" Bowen said enthusiastically.

The boy shrugged. "I take it that you—the older generation— are responsible for *this*, for the way we live, for—"

"Sure, why not?" Ginsberg said, and leaning forward toward the boy, he put his fingertips together and touched them to his forehead, to signify that he recognized and respected the presence of another sentient being in the meditation room.

"The great Ginsberg won't even let me finish," the boy complained.

Bowen jumped up. "Hey, man, we don't get nasty here," he said.

"What do you want to hurt my feelings for anyway?" Ginsberg asked the boy. He sounded serious.

Snyder started laughing. "Don't take it all out on Allen," he said. "This has been going on since the Stone Age. Why, there's a chain of us going back to the late Paleolithic. Like Whitman and Jeffers. *They* had good scenes going."

"The only thing is that more people love and kiss and touch now," Ginsberg said.

"And more people kill and bomb—that's the *other* side of Kali," Bowen broken in. He sounded astonished at his insight.

"But the other side of Kali is Parvati, and she's beautiful, and dances," a girl in an orange-feather gown called out from the bottom of a pile of people.

"It's all one, baby," Bowen philosophized.

Ginsberg stood up, stretching. Leary had just walked in with the early edition of the next day's San Francisco *Chronicle* and handed it to him. On the front page, over a picture of the Be-In, was the headline HIPPIES RUN WILD.

"That's ridiculous," Ginsberg said, when he had finished reading their reviews. "Like it was an aesthetically very good scene. They should have sent an art critic."

"It's a bad bag, reporting," Snyder mused. "Somehow I don't think it's possible to be in that bag and get anywhere, spiritually speaking."

Ginsberg said that, nevertheless, he had "better straighten things out." He left the meditators debating the spiritual pitfalls of journalism, and down the hall in Bowen's studio, where there was another telephone, he dialed the *Chronicle* and asked for the night editor. Maretta trailed in after him, holding a cigarette. He took a long weary puff.

"What is this nonsense about hippies running wild?" Ginsberg said, scolding the night editor. "Your story has the kind of inaccuracy of tone and language that's *poisoning* the community. Is *that* what you want to do?" He proceeded to dissect the story, word by word. "What do you mean nobody *told* you that?" he said. "What kind of reporting is *that*?"

"We sent our hippie-est reporter," the night editor said.

"I don't know what kind of hippies you've got over there at *your* place," Ginsberg said, chuckling. "Besides, what is this hippie business? What does 'hippie' mean anyway? These kids aren't hippies—they're *seekers*. Today was a serious religious occasion."

"Fucking right it was," Maretta remarked. Ginsberg gave her a hug. He told the night editor to expect him early Monday morning for a talk with the reporter about an accurate follow-up.

The editor agreed.

"Well, peace," Ginsberg said.

Chapter 4

Ginsberg was twenty-seven when he came to San Francisco for the first time, and he had thirty borrowed dollars in his pocket, an introduction from William Carlos Williams to Kenneth Rexroth, and a modest reputation in the market-research business as a young man who would go far if he ever kept a job. It was 1953, and no one in San Francisco then had ever heard of him. He had been living in New York since the day in 1944 that he enrolled at Columbia on a small scholarship and a stipend from the Paterson, New Jersey, Young Men's Hebrew Association. He was, for all practical purposes, unpublished. And the other writers he knew—Ginsberg had lived with William Burroughs, off and on, for years, and Jack Kerouac and Corso were his closest friends —were all based on the East Coast.

"It was like a big prophecy, taking off for California," Ginsberg has said. "Like I had passed one season of my life and it was time to start all over again." He spent a year getting there. He hitchhiked to Florida, hopped a plane to Cuba, decided to explore the Yucatán—"Like Shelley in Italy, I was busy poking around big history-less Mayan ruins and wandering all over alone, absorbing that kind of antiquity and sense of transience and thinking up big long poems about native grounds"—and ended up on a jungle cocoa *finca* near the Guatemalan border, visiting a retired Tarzan-movie Jane whom he had met on a roof comb at one of the Palenque ruins. When he finally did reach California, after six months at the *finca*, he headed for San Jose to see his friend Neal Cassady, a sometime railroad brakeman who liked memorizing Proust and reading Kant before bed. Cassady was the prototype for Dean Moriarity in Kerouac's *On the Road,* and he was revered by Kerouac, Ginsberg, and their friends as a kind of savant-in-the-raw. (He later teamed up with the novelist Ken Kesey, as the driver of Kesey's "Psychedelic Bus," a paisleyed piece of old machinery that carried the writer and his followers, who called themselves Merry Pranksters, on an endless holiday up and down the West Coast. In Mexico, in February of 1968, he took a lethal combination of liquor and barbiturates and was found dead on a railroad track outside of San Miguel de Allende). Ginsberg moved in with Cassady and Cassady's wife—he had made up his mind to abandon market research for railroading, which paid more in those days, but no one would hire him—and stayed, he says, until Mrs. Cassady "got a little bugged." Cassady dropped him off in San Francisco.

Ginsberg settled down in a six-dollar-a-week room in a North Beach transients' hotel, on Broadway and Columbus. It was around the corner from Lawrence Ferlinghetti's bookstore, City Lights, and Ginsberg, having taken a stack of his poems over to Ferlinghetti and introduced himself, spent his first few weeks in town there, getting to know the local poets. Then he happened to find both a job, at a small market-research firm called Towne-Oller, and a girl friend, and soon he and the girl were installed in what he says was an appropriately executive apartment on Nob Hill. After a year of keeping house and plotting out the effects of cold-cream and tooth-paste advertising campaigns on supermarket sales, Ginsberg concluded that the time had come to ask a psychiatrist why he seemed to be so dissatisfied with doing both. He began shopping around for a doctor—trying, he says, to forget the fact that, asking roughly the same question, he already had run through a number of psychoanalysts in New York. The first New York analyst, who was a Reikian, had dismissed Ginsberg for smoking marijuana against doctor's orders. Ginsberg wanted to go back to him some months later, after having an auditory hallucination of William Blake reading "Ah! Sun-Flower," but he says that when he phoned the doctor and said, "Look, I have to see you—William Blake is in my room," the doctor shouted, "You must be crazy," and immediately hung up on him. The next psychiatrist, who was assigned to Ginsberg during an eight-month visit he paid to the Psychiatric Institute at the Columbia-Presbyterian Medical Center on what he now refers to as "my leave of absence from college," apparently felt the same way: "In our first week's conversation," Ginsberg says, "I was trying to explain to him where I was at, and I said, 'It's like the telephone is alive.' Now, had he been a doctor of any kind of wit, like they had in the old days, he would have said, 'And what does the telephone say, Allen?' But instead he got annoyed and stamped his foot and said, 'The telephone is *not* alive.' So he didn't know where I was at at all." The last of the Institute doctors was a young Freudian, starting out in practice, and he and Ginsberg got along. "He had my diagnosis changed from psychotic or schizophrenic or something terrible like that to 'extreme but socially average neurosis,' which gave me a lot of confidence, because ever since then I've had formal credentials of not being insane," Ginsberg says. But the doctor got married, moved to Park Avenue, raised his rates from seven-fifty an hour to twenty-five, and told Ginsberg to get a better job.

It was the San Francisco doctor, a psychiatrist named Philip Hicks, who "gave me the authority, so to speak, to be myself," Ginsberg says. "I had like a beautiful conversation with him one day, and the key thing I said was that I was dissatisfied with what I was doing, I was very unsure of myself. So he said, 'What would you like to do? What *is* your desire, really?' I said, 'Doctor, I don't think you're going to find this very healthy and clear, but I really would like to stop working forever—never work again, never do anything like the kind of work I'm doing now— and do nothing but write poetry and have leisure to spend the day outdoors and go to museums and see friends. And I'd like to keep living with someone—maybe even a man—and explore relationships that way. And cultivate my perceptions, cultivate the visionary thing in me. Just a literary and quiet city-hermit existence.' Then *he* said, 'Well, why don't you?' It was the last thing I expected him to say. I asked him what the American Psychoanalytic Association would say about *that*, and he said, 'There's no party line, no red book on how people are supposed to live. If that is what you really feel would please you, what in the world is stopping you from doing it?' So I said that the only thing stopping me was my being in psychoanalysis and feeling that that kind of screwy thinking wasn't exactly contributing toward my general development, and he said that it obviously was contributing toward *something*, if it was what I wanted to do with my life. So that was really delightful, getting that kind of talk from an analyst. The thing I suddenly was beginning to realize about Hicks was that he actually liked me and wanted to see me pleased and happy and free to develop in my *own* way, and I was curious about this and said, 'But this is so far distinct from your way of life. Don't you feel any conflict?' He kind of shrugged and said, 'No, I'*m* happy with what I'm doing, and I don't see any reason for *you* not to be happy with what you do.' Like he just was a very good person, a good human being, and I guess that's what I had needed all along."

Ginsberg went home that night and drafted a report on the

economic advantages of installing a small I.B.M. machine at Towne-Oller, to replace himself and his two secretaries. He says that Mr. Towne and Mr. Oller were moved by his consideration and ingenuity, which, as it turned out, would save them seven hundred dollars a month. They obligingly fired him, to specifications, with a signed statement to the effect that Ginsberg was the unfortunate victim of technological progress. Ginsberg began collecing forty dollars a week in unemployment checks. Soon after that, he met Peter Orlovsky.

Orlovsky was the son of a White Russian cavalry officer who had gone AWOL and ended up in lower Manhattan making silk-screen ties. The family tie loft was a Dickensian sort of place, according to Orlovsky—grim, dank, and run entirely with forced labor in the form of the Orlovsky children. Orlovsky, who was not enthusiastic about ties in the best of circumstances, left it at sixteen to clean the geriatric wards of a mental hospital nearby. He was drafted at eighteen, assigned to Presidio, an Army base in San Francisco, and eventually presented with a medical discharge. Many years later, at a literary cocktail party in Chicago, he sized himself up with the introduction, "I'm Peter Orlovsky. I'm very fine and happy and crazy as a wildflower." His only autobiography, a paragraph written in 1960 for a poetry anthologer, reads: "Grew up with dirty feet & giggles. Cant stand dust so pick my nose. Trouble in school: always thinking dreaming sad mistry problems . . . Love pretzels & cant remember dreams any more. Will somebody please buy me mountain with a cave up there. I dont speack any more. Wanted to be a farmer went to high school for that & worked hard, hard, I tell you, very hard, you'd be amazed. Did weight lifting with bus stops. Got to enjoy burnt bacon with mothers help. Stare at my feet to much & need to undue paroniac suden clowds. Enjoy mopping floors, cleaning up cat vommit. Enjoy swinning underwater. I want the moon for fun. Getting to enjoy blank mind state, especially in tub . . . This summer got to like flies tickleing nose & face. I demand piss to be sold on the market, it would help people to get to know eachother. I.Q. 90 in school, now specialized I.Q. is thousands."

When Ginsberg discovered him, around Christmas of 1954, Orlovsky was twenty-one. "I had wandered out to Foster's Cafeteria that night," as Ginsberg tells the story, "and got talking to a painter named Robert La Vigne and after a while he asked me over to his house to take a look at his things. There was this giant picture there, over the fireplace, a very beautiful portrait of Peter, naked, with a Greek kind of drapery around him. Kind of a Matisse style of painting, very sexy and very innocent. And something happened sort of between me and it; that is, like I fell in love with it, and so I was delighted a few minutes later when Peter actually walked in the room—he was a sophomore at some local junior college—with his schoolbooks under his arm. We had a long, long, long beautiful talk. It was like there was a great deal of correspondence between our experiences. His brother's in the madhouse like *my* mother had been, his father and mother separated just like mine, his Russian background, and then this particular visionary thing he told me about that was so beautiful. That at the height of his depression in San Francisco he was walking toward school and had started weeping, and that the trees on the street had all bowed to him. It reminded me of my Blake thing, so like right away we found a mutual key, which was very ethereal, talking about dreams and the nature of consciousness and about what we were seeking, and discovering that we were more or less seeking to exchange souls with each other . . . Then one night a while later we all went down to North Beach together and got a little drunk, and La Vigne, who had been Peter's lover, said that he and Peter were breaking up, and that he liked Peter, and would I take over for him because Peter needed someone and he knew that Peter liked me. I said, 'Now wait a minute! What are you proposing? My heart is broken. This is too beautiful to be true.' So there was a very strange scene going, with La Vigne invoking my genii for Peter and talking to Peter, and Peter saying that he wasn't sure, that like he wanted to *know* me more. There wasn't anything vulgar about it. It was very beautiful, totally unlike a New York faggot situation. It was like some sort of very idealized happy Dostoevskian confrontation of souls . . . Then—at about three one morning in one of the cafeterias downtown—we finally made a kind of vow. It was that I owned his body and soul and he owned my body and soul. Total interpossession was what we decided. It was a very strange, illuminating subjective moment, with the burden of fear and doubt falling off for both of us. Everything lit up. It was a *great* moment . . . Now my *girl* friend—I wasn't living with her any more but I was still ardent about her and that for me was a relief—she got cold and annoyed at me for some reason that I couldn't make out. It was as if my thing with men had really bugged her, put her off. I was like saying, Why don't we *all* go to bed together, but for some reason she got mad at that. She came over to the new apartment I had taken with Peter and threw a fit one night. She broke my fireplace, told me I was a wretch and a disgusting queer and a monster. She began acting in such a wounded hysterical way that I didn't know how to react to it, actually. Here I wanted a quiet, community thing, just a little household community, but that apparently just struck some bad note in her. It was a shame, really, because Peter was bringing chicks home, so there were a lot of nice orgies going on. We didn't have any agreement about them, or anything like that. Just a very clever understanding that whichever of us desired anybody else and wanted to make it—fine. So it worked out well, much better than any big jealous arrangement. Actually I think the terms of the thing were that he give me the tolerance and love I needed until I finally felt secure enough to make it successfully with girls too, until all *my* sensitivity and shyness and anxiety and fears about being unlovable were totally wiped out. *That*, in return for my education and my mysticism and whatever I had picked up about life. Those were the conditions of the marriage, so to speak."

Ginsberg finished the first part of "Howl" in an apartment he took with Orlovsky on Montgomery Street. It was only a few blocks from the center of North Beach, and Ginsberg liked the contact he had there with the writers, artists, and hangers-on who were beginning to arrive in shaggy mass migrations and were destined to give the neighborhood five years of notoriety as a Beat paradise. (North Beach, on the fringes of Chinatown, is at the moment playing commercial host to San Francisco's topless night clubs, topless shoeshine parlors, topless fortune tellers, topless newsgirls, and topless self-styled lay psychiatrists, and looks something like a small Times Square. A few aging alcoholic *littérateurs* are still around, but Ferlinghetti's excellent bookstore is North Beach's only thriving reminder of the old Beat scene.) The young poets, especially, had been settling down in San Francisco, with North Beach as their headquarters. When Ginsberg arrived, Jack Spicer, Philip Lamantia, Edward Dorn, Lew Welch, Philip Whalen, and Michael McClure, as well as the older writers—Ferlinghetti, Rexroth, and Robert Duncan— were already here. They had been drawn by what Ginsberg calls "the long honorable San Francisco tradition of Bohemian-Buddhist-Wobbly-mystical-anarchist social involvement and a local literary consciousness in terms of Western woodsmanship and a kind of competent communal outdoor life." Most of them were linked by networks of friendship and correspondence to their contemporaries on the East Coast—especially to the new Black Mountain poets and *their* mentor, Charles Olson—and, like Ginsberg, preferred Williams to Eliot and wanted to write in the rhythms of regional American speech. Ginsberg, who decided to learn something about prosody for the sake of his own poetry and "maybe arrive at some understanding of what we were *all* doing in terms of what could be done," enrolled in the graduate school at Berkeley when the fall semester began. To pay tuition, he took a job, nights, as a busboy at Robbie's Cafeteria on Telegraph Avenue and then rented a one-room cottage in the neighborhood to use during the week when he was working late. Snyder, who was also at the graduate school studying Chinese and Japanese, lived near Ginsberg in a hut on the edge of someone's backyard. Ginsberg, walking over to the hut one day to introduce himself as a fellow poet, discovered Snyder in Zen meditation—an occupation that caught his fancy, as did Snyder's declaration that he too practiced Williams' poetic dictum, "No ideas but in things."

Ginsberg remembers that Snyder had a hibachi and a recipe for horse meat sukiyaki. "It tasted very good with some kind of sweet sugar and vinegar sauce he made," Ginsberg says. "We'd have parties at the cottage at night and run around naked in the backyard, looking like fauns, and all the girls in the neighborhood would come over. During the day, though, it was like a very funny little Buddhist hermits' retreat. We'd garden and carve poems on trees and sit and talk and meditate like a bunch of slightly crazy Japanese mountain monks. Kerouac was with us then—he'd come out to the Coast that winter for a visit—and Jack, it turned out, was a big learned Buddhist, like Gary, something I hadn't realized before. Like he'd read terrifically for about four years in all the important texts and knew all about the *Paramita Sutra* and the significance of the Vows and the Refuges. His *Dharma Bums*, which was about our scene in Berkeley, was actually a very scholarly esoteric Buddhist book. He wasn't on the Zen Mahayana Buddhist kick that Gary was. Mostly, he knew the early Hinayana Buddhism. So he was like a very unique cat—a French Canadian Hinayana Buddhist Beat Catholic savant."

Years before, over a friendly beer in New York, Kerouac inadvertently had coined the phrase "the Beat Generation," and he was properly on hand in San Francisco for what one chronicler called its "birth trauma"—the night that Ginsberg read "Howl" for the first time. Ginsberg had arranged the reading for Wally Hedrick, a painter who had opened an artists' cooperative called the Six Gallery, and wanted to get it off to what Ginsberg modestly calls "a lively start." Ginsberg had invited Snyder, Whalen, Lamantia, and McClure to read with him, persuaded Rexroth to introduce them, and mailed out a few hundred mimeographed postcards, written in what he refers to as "real classical poetic public discourse gaiety style," promising everyone who came free wine, free flowers, and a "Happy Apocalypse." Ginsberg's friends read first, to a house full of poets, painters, local aficionados, and ardent relatives. Kerouac, Cassady, Orlovsky, Rexroth, and Ferlinghetti were stationed around the gallery, for moral support, with Kerouac in charge of getting everybody else in the audience efficiently and enthusiastically drunk.

"I read last, and I was *very* drunk," Ginsberg says now, "and I gave a very wild, funny, tearful reading of the first part of 'Howl.' Like I really felt shame and power reading it, and every time I'd finish a long line Kerouac would shout, 'Yeah!' or 'So there!' or 'Correct!' or some little phrase, which added a kind of extra note of bop humor to the whole thing. It was like a jam session, and I was very astounded because 'Howl' was a big, long poem and yet everybody seemed to understand and at the same time to sympathize with it. Like this was the end of the McCarthy scene, and here I was talking about super-Communist pamphlets on Union Square and the national Golgotha and the Fascists and all the things that turned out to be implicit in a sort of social community revolution that was actually going on. The evening ended up with everybody absolutely radiant and happy, with talk and kissing and later on big happy orgies of poets. It was an *ideal* evening, and I felt so proud and pleased and happy with the sense of—the sense of 'at last a community,' for one thing. Jack said, 'Ginsberg, this poem "Howl" will make you famous in San Francisco,' but Rexroth said, 'No, this poem will make you famous from bridge to bridge,' which sounded like hyperbole, but I guess it did."

Chapter 5

Late one morning after the Human Be-In, Ginsberg was stretched out on an Army-surplus sleeping bag in the front parlor of a vast and dilapidated Victorian flat off lower Divisadero Street, clipping hippie news from the San Francisco *Chronicle* and waiting for Maretta and the Orlovskys to get dressed for a walk to see A. C. Bhaktivedanta, the new neighborhood swami. He had rented the apartment for the month that they were planning to spend in San Francisco and had just moved in the day before with the family knapsacks, suitcases, and sleeping bags, a few borrowed mattresses, and Maretta's portable shrine. The former tenants, a pair of dope pushers who had decided that a change of address, if not cities, was appropriate, had dropped by to offer Ginsberg their old pots and pans and a few tables and chairs—they would be traveling light, they said—and to leave a farewell note for their customers taped to the stairwell, and they had stayed for a few hours, helping Orlovsky scrub down all the rooms. The apartment still smelled of ammonia, and Ginsberg had said earlier that he would be perfectly content with the place were it not for the fact that several hundred cockroaches were in permanent residence there. The pushers had offered their experienced advice on roach control in the apartment, but Orlovsky, who does not believe in murder, had interceded on behalf of the bugs. At the moment, two of them were crawling toward the sleeping bag. Ginsberg lifted one of his sandals with a menacing look, but when he heard Orlovsky in the kitchen begin chattering compassionately to some of the roaches *there*—"Now, now, sweeties, that's not *your* teacup"—Ginsberg shrugged sheepishly, tossed the sandal aside, and got up instead. He was sitting at a rickety wooden table by the window, watching cars pull in and out of a filling station across the street, when Maretta walked in with two cups of coffee and some Fig Newtons. Maretta was still in her pajamas; she said that Julius had been soaking in the bathtub for half an hour and showed no interest in getting out. While Ginsberg went to retrieve him, Maretta, apparently giving up on a bath, changed into a pair of baggy black ski pants and a black sweater, braided her long blond hair into two pigtails, and began outlining her eyes with kohl at a broken mirror on an old marble mantelpiece.

"You missed a groovy night last night," Ginsberg said, running back into the room to kiss Maretta good morning. "I was wandering around Haight Street—it was maybe two o'clock—and hit on two beautiful kids in the Drugstore Café. Brothers. Mexican or Puerto Rican, and both high on LSD."

Maretta listened attentively while continuing with her eyelids.

"I must have spent at least four hours talking to them," Ginsberg went on. "They were *beautiful*. Like one of them told me, 'You know, that Leary guy's slogan is all wrong—it should be drop out, turn on, and *then* tune in.' I asked him what he meant and he said, 'America was always supposed to be a temple, so let's tune into it, let's make it plastic and holy, not run away from it.' A *kid* said that. Then they told me that their high school was impossible, so I asked them what they were interested in learning. And the younger kid said, 'Eastern religion, astronomy, astrology, and personal relations as applicable to the society.' "

"Personal relations?" Maretta said.

"I asked him if he meant sociology," Ginsberg said, "and the kid said yeah, that you could call it that."

"Anything else?" Maretta asked, arranging her shawl over her pigtails.

"Well, at about six-thirty in the morning we went over to Swami Bhaktivedanta's space station for some chanting and a little Krishna consciousness," Ginsberg said. "There were about thirty or forty people there, all chanting *Hare Krishna* to this new tune they've made up, just for mornings. One kid got like a little freaked out by the scene at first, but then he relaxed, and afterward he told me, 'You know, at first I thought, What *is* this? But then suddenly I realized I was just not grooving with where I was. I wasn't being where I was.' " Ginsberg shook his head. "And this was a *kid*."

"You get laid?" Maretta asked cheerfully.

Ginsberg shook his head. "I liked those kids too much—I just wanted to talk."

"*I* did," Maretta said.

Ginsberg gave her a hug. "Good for you," he said. Just then Peter Orlovsky burst in and shouted, "Alrighty, alrighty, everybody out of here!" Orlovsky was tall, rippling, and entirely elastic, and while Ginsberg and Maretta gulped down their coffee, he sprang around the room with his dustcloth like a somewhat distracted kangaroo. He had put on a new sleeveless jersey for the walk and had tied his mane of long brown hair back into a neat ponytail with a red ribbon, but his eyes were bleary and there was several days' growth of stubble on his chin. Ginsberg, who looked worried, asked Orlovsky if he had "taken" anything.

By way of a reply, Orlovsky let out a whoop, seized a big red Indian harmonium from the mantelpiece, let out a whoop and fled down the stairs and out onto the sidewalk, where he started hopping up and down. He was chirping to some pigeons and fiddling with the harmonium, when Ginsberg came out to find him. Maretta followed in a minute, leading Julius by the hand. Peter gently ruffled his brother's crew cut and then, skipping ahead barefoot, led the way down the block to Haight Street.

Divisadero, as it approaches Haight, is the main street of an old Negro neighborhood that was just beginning to absorb the hippie overflow. It was lined with storefront churches—Ginsberg's block had three—and Ginsberg ducked into most of them, asking when services were and saying "Om" to the ministers. Then he stopped with his friends to do some shopping in a Haitian establishment that was selling out chocolate crucifixes and bottles of pink and blue anointing oil labeled "Love," "Peace," "John the Conqueror," and "U.C." The preacher behind the counter told Ginsberg that U.C. stood for "uncrossing" and that the oil was used by the faithful whenever they were "all crossed up." Ginsberg bought some, and after the preacher pointed out that Maretta was putting out her cigarettes in his holy water, Ginsberg stocked up on a supply of Peace oil, too. By the time the group had turned the corner onto Haight Street, five strangers had been anointed on their foreheads with Peace oil and three more preventatively uncrossed.

On Haight Street, people began recognizing Ginsberg. Boys and girls who were strolling in front of the psychedelic shops, playing their flutes and harmonicas, called "Hi, Allen" and "Hare Krishna" as Ginsberg and his friends passed. Ginsberg had a Uher tape recorder—it was a Christmas present from Bob Dylan—in his purple book bag, and he turned it on whenever a sound or a piece of conversation on the street appealed to him.

Outside the Drugstore Café, where they were going to have some lunch, several hippies were chatting about Mao Tse-tung. Ginsberg walked up to them.

"I don't know," one beaded young man was saying, "I just sort of *prefer* Mao to the others."

"Well, there must be *something* about him that makes him so obnoxious," Ginsberg said.

"Mao is a meat-eater, I bet," another young man, apparently an anti-Maoist, broke in.

"Mao does *not* eat meat," said the first young man.

"Come on, man, he eats meat—and I bet he drinks, too," the anti-Mao man shouted.

"It's well known that Mao consults *I Ching,* so how can someone dig *I Ching* and still be a meat-eater?" the first boy shouted back.

"I bet Mao's never even taken acid," the anti-Mao man said firmly, as a final statement. Everybody gasped.

Ginsberg wagged his finger. "Ginsberg say 'Beware of all governments,'" he told them. "Russia *and* the U.S. *and* China all abhor the blushing peony." He turned to Julius, who had been bundled up in a huge tweed overcoat and was looking cross. "Isn't that right, Julius?"

Julius nodded solemnly.

Ginsberg took his hand and said, "Come on, Julie, let's hit the Drugstore."

The Drugstore, which happened to be the most popular cafeteria on Haight Street at the moment, was an enormous and ornate old corner store loft, with a display of antique apothecary bottles and a practically resident clientele in various stages of hallucination and enlightenment. Out of respect to the clientele, which kept the Drugstore open for a twenty-four-hour day, it was decorated entirely in paisley, a predominantly pink-and-purple

Day-Glo paisley, which covered the walls, the tabletops, the cash registers, and the ties, belts, and chefs' hats of the young men who dished out the house specialty—cold macaroni salad in paper cups—at a long counter at the far end of the room.

Ginsberg and his friends waited in line at the counter behind about a dozen hippies, one of whom said that he had been "hanging around digging the food" since the previous evening. Ginsberg ordered a hamburger, and when it arrived, the hippie said that for a hamburger it was really beautiful. Maretta and the Orlovskys took macaroni.

As soon as the group was settled at a table by the windows, Ginsberg switched on his Uher and described the scene: "A lot of bottles. Julius is licking his lips. Peter oils himself with Peace oil. Barbra Streisand sings 'Happy Days Are Here Again.' " He then entered a few spur-of-the-moment poetic thoughts. "Reagan, Mister Fascist, should *pay* people to go to school," Ginsberg was saying when a feverish-looking young man ran up and began shaking him.

"Hey, Allen, Allen, Allen, remember me?" the young man shouted into Ginsberg's ear. "It's Frank, Frank. Remember?"

"Come on, take it easy, calm down," Ginsberg said softly, pulling over a chair from the next table and motioning to Frank, whom he had never seen before, to sit down. Then he held out his microphone. "What do you think about this?" he asked. "The proposal is that the government *pay* people to go to school."

"Yeah, man, I'd go to school but I don't know how I'm gonna get out of the snake pit with Reagan in," Frank said.

"You in the hospital?" Ginsberg asked.

"They let me out for the day, but they've had me for five years," Frank said. "They call it"—he thought for a moment —"chronic undifferentiated schizophrenic reaction."

Orlovsky leapt out of his chair and peered at Frank. "Boy, you sure sound normal to me," he said.

"No, I'm not normal," Frank said. "My psychiatrist—that rat

fink—he called me a nonconformist." He turned to Ginsberg.
"Allen, do *you* think I'm a nonconformist?"

Ginsberg shrugged. "How should I know?"

"Do you think I'm *abominable*?" Frank asked.

"You're not abominable," Ginsberg said, laughing. "You just
ask too many questions."

"I'm abominable," Frank said.

Ginsberg thought for a minute, and then made a mudra for
expelling demons over Frank's head.

Frank asked what he was doing.

Ginsberg replied that he was making a signal. "It's like an
all-right sign," Ginsberg said. "Like I hope you're all right."

"Bless you," Frank said.

Ginsberg looked surprised. "Bless *you*," Ginsberg said.

Ginsberg stayed on at the Drugstore for about an hour. He
grilled Frank on conditions at the state mental hospital in
Napa, where the young man was apparently committed. Then
he conferred with a delegation of reclaimed Hell's Angels on the
problems involved in reclaiming policemen; talked to a pair of
"psychedelic prospectors" from the High Sierras—they were in
town recruiting hippies for their Love Goldmining Cooperative—
about the possibility of a mass Haight-Ashbury migration to
whatever was left there of the free Homestead Act land; and
finally he listened to the editor of the San Francisco *Oracle*, the
hippies' neighborhood paper, weigh the astrological pros and
cons of coming out with a new issue while Aquarius was descend-
ing. Peter Orlovsky, having purchased several more cups of macaroni salad, kept busy skipping back and forth across the cafeteria,
urging his macaroni on everyone he thought looked underfed.
Maretta was out of cigarettes, and eventually she began making
the rounds of likely-looking tables, trying to barter some homemade fudge at the rate of two squares to one joint. Nobody took
Maretta up on her offer—"Man, that's the first time anyone ever
asked me *that*, even the police," one boy said admiringly—but

by the time she left to pay her respects to the Swami, everyone agreed that Maretta was the most original businesswoman to have hit the Haight-Ashbury in quite a while.

A. C. Bhaktivedanta, Swami, had just moved to San Francisco from his ashram and "International Headquarters" on the Lower East Side of New York, where he had made modest headlines by conducting mass Sunday kirtans in Tompkins Square Park, and where he had managed to convert a number of young men to a state of celibacy, vegetarianism, and devotion called Krishna Consciousness. Ginsberg knew the Swami from New York. They were neighbors of sorts, and the Swami had helped him out with some of the finer points of Bhakti yoga, a discipline which translates roughly as "adoration from the heart yoga," which consisted, for the Swami, of singing the Hindu mantra *Hare Krishna* all day long, and which the Swami believed to be the only sensible way, yogically speaking, of coping with reality in troubled times. Earlier that winter, out of friendship for Ginsberg, the Swami had also consented to bring his local disciples to a peace benefit at an Egyptian dance hall on West Fifty-second Street, where they appeared as the Hare Krishna Singers and, under the deceptive strobe lights, were mistaken by many for a new raga-rock group. Consequently, when the Swami's plane set down in San Francisco, Ginsberg had been waiting at the airport with a bunch of chrysanthemums, in the company of some forty Kirshna-worshipers who shouted *"Hare Krishna Hare Krishna Krishna Krishna Hare Hare Hare Rama Hare Rama Rama Rama Hare Hare"* and threw flower petals as the old Indian gentleman walked from Arrivals to Baggage, nodding pontifically and blessing travelers. By now, Ginsberg was in the habit of dropping by the Swami's new ashram for some warm-up chanting on his free afternoons.

"You know what the Swami told me yesterday?" Ginsberg said to Maretta as they walked toward the ashram, which was a couple of blocks south of Haight on Frederick Street. "He said, '*I'm* going to die soon. People follow you. *You* continue my work, please.' "

Maretta stared at Ginsberg. The Swami was known to have a rather uncharitable opinion of meat, spirits, marijuana, psychedelics, coffee, tea, tobacco, sex, and thinking about sex, among other things, and Maretta said she was wondering what Ginsberg planned to do about all of them.

"I said, 'Not me, Swami. I still smoke cigarettes,' " Ginsberg replied. "I told him that if it would help matters I'd promise to sing *Hare Krishna* every night before bed for the rest of my life."

"That's telling him, Ginzy," Peter Orlovsky, who had run ahead, called over his shoulder.

Ginsberg grinned, but Maretta, who looked particularly thoughtful, said that she had had similar ethical problems regarding her Buddhist vows.

"There's the vow to avoid intoxicants as beclouding the mind," Maretta said, "which you might say I break all the time with hashish. That bothered me for a bit in India, but I thought about it and figured that since I didn't *think* about hash as an intoxicant, and I didn't use it to get beclouded precisely, then, man, I wasn't breaking any vows." She looked inquiringly at Ginsberg, who said "*Om*" and burst out laughing.

They had just turned into a long bleak street of warehouses, tenements, and empty lots where the Swami was running his ashram in an abandoned storefront, and they ran to catch up with the Orlovskys, who were already waiting at the door. With a hearty "*Hare Krishna*," a tall, full-bearded young man in blue jeans, a pea jacket, and bright red beads let them into a long, narrow room with a makeshift altar at the far end, and above it, a glaring portrait of a bright blue Krishna and Radha, his bride. The altar, a wobbly wooden table draped with a fringed Indian shawl, was banked with white lilies and reeked of burning incense and scented candles. The day's offerings—a shaft of wheat, half a loaf of rice-flour bread, a box of saltines, two candles, and a pair of finger cymbals—were piled before it on a tattered oriental rug. Maretta walked to the altar, blessed everything, and added her unbartered fudge squares to the pile. Ginsberg and Orlovsky leafed through the latest International Society for Krishna Consciousness, Inc., literature, which was on a shelf by the door. There were a number of pamphlets by the Swami, including "Stay High Forever—No More Coming Down: Practice Krishna Consciousness" and "Swami Bhaktivedanta Gives You the Peace Formula," as well as several sets of the first three published volumes of the Swami's masterwork—an annotated translation of the *Srimad Bhagwatan,* which is a sixty-volume commentary by Krishna Daipayana Vyas on the *Vedanta Sutra.* The young man in the pea jacket assured Ginsberg that the Swami's recent masterpiece "Who Is Crazy?" would be back from the printers late that afternoon.

"You one of the Swami's boys?" Ginsberg asked him.

The young man looked proud. He was "an old disciple from New York," he said, and his name, until the happy day when he would earn an Indian name, was Lefkowitz. "The Swami showed me that there was only one god and that god was Krishna," Lefkowitz said.

"What about Siva, or Rama?" Ginsberg asked. "It gets me when the Swami puts *them* down. I guess I don't always agree with the Swami. He keeps *insisting* on things." Ginsberg shrugged. He told Lefkowitz that he was having trouble, as it was, calling Bhaktivedanta "the Swami." In New York, owing to the presence of a rival Hindu holy man on West End Avenue, Bhaktivedanta was referred to by his friends as "the Downtown Swami."

"One Swami is better, like one god," Lefkowitz said. Then he motioned Ginsberg and Peter over to the rug. Another one of the Swami's disciples, wearing red beads like Lefkowitz's, had emerged from a kitchen in the back with a large bowl of apple sauce and a pitcher of warm milk and floating banana slices, and Lefkowitz pushed aside some offerings to make room for the food. Ginsberg sampled the apple sauce, and said it was excellent. He had eaten apple sauce several times at the storefront next door, where the local chapter of psychedelic social workers called Diggers dispensed free food, clothes, and lodging to indigent hippies, but, he told Lefkowitz, he was going to eat at the Swami's, where the apple sauce was better, from now on.

"We serve free lunch every day, too," Lefkowitz said. "You get a lot of people in that way. The Diggers understand. One of them told me, 'If a guy comes in for lunch who's more on your path than ours, we always send him right over to you.' "

At the mention of lunch, Orlovsky whipped a rag out of the back pocket of his jeans and announced that he was going to clean the Swami's kitchen immediately. Lefkowitz told him to sit down. He said that there were already four disciples on kitchen duty, cooking and cleaning according to the three hundred recipes in their sacred cookbook, the *Chaitanya Tantra*, which was written by Krishna in one of his incarnations in the fifteenth century.

"That what you do all day, sweetie, cook and chant?" Orlovsky asked him. "No girls?"

Lefkowitz shook his head.

"That's pretty hard when you're young." Orlovsky was sympathetic.

"I have Krishna," Lefkowitz said.

Ginsberg looked up from his plate of apple sauce. "Don't you get tired of singing *Hare Krishna* all day long?" he said.

Lefkowitz said that he found the suggestion astonishing.

"Well, any changes in you yet?" Ginsberg went on. "Like outside the normal limits of consciousness?"

"Yes," Lefkowitz replied. "Krishna consciousness. Consciousness of God within me."

Julius laughed. It was his first sound in a week.

"You think he's right, Julie?" Ginsberg said gently, getting up from the rug and walking over to where Julius was standing, all by himself, against a wall. Julius turned away.

"Julius may be higher than all of us," Ginsberg told Lefkowitz, who was staring at them.

"He's the family shaman, huh?" Lefkowitz said.

"Yeah, maybe he's Krishna." Ginsberg laughed, and tapped Julius on the shoulder. "You like Krishna, Julie?"

"Why should anybody not like Krishna?" a voice behind them snapped.

Ginsberg turned around and then bowed. Swami Bhaktivedanta was standing in the kitchen door, trailing a long strand of beads and dressed for evening kirtan in a saffron robe, a shrimp-pink cardigan, and a pair of white sweatsocks. Lefkowitz leapt up to escort him to the rug, where the Swami proceeded to lower himself into a lotus pose. The Swami was tiny. He had sharp, bulging eyes and a livid mouth, and his head, which was shaved smooth and scrubbed, glowed under the yellow bulbs that lit the room. Ginsberg gave him a comradely slap on the knee and said, "Hi, Swami, *Hare Krishna.*"

The Swami grunted. He had been chanting for the last six hours, he said, but there had been so many interruptions that he was several thousand *Hare Krishnas* short of his goal of a hundred thousand a day.

"My teacher, *three* hundred thousand times a day he said *Hare Krishna,*" the old man said, sighing.

Ginsberg agreed that that was fast chanting. "How do you keep track?" he said.

Bhaktivedanta held up his beads. "There are one hundred and eight beads. One bead for each *Hare Krishna*; that is to say, one thousand two hundred twenty-eight *Hare Krishnas* for the whole circle. Then I begin again."

Ginsberg looked confused.

"I will explain another way," the Swami said. "Six hours is record for one hundred thousand *Hare Krishnas.* That is sixteen thousand six hundred sixty-six *Hare Krishnas* more or less in one hour, which is—let me see—two thousand seven hundred seventy-seven more or less in ten minutes." He beamed at Ginsberg. "Now you understand."

Ginsberg threw up his hands. "You know, the Swami should really see the spectacle of the rock dancing here," he said, turning to Lefkowitz. The Swami was about to make his San Francisco debut at a combination Hindu light show and mass Chant-In at one of the local psychedelic-rock ballrooms, and there were rumors on Haight Street that he was planning to flee immediately after his act to avoid heretical contact with the Quicksilver Messenger Service and the Grateful Dead, who were booked to follow him.

Lefkowitz frowned. "Oh, he'll see it, he can't help but see it."

"Come on, now," Ginsberg said. "It might be useful for the Swami. Rock-and-roll is very high here. Very happy. It's like a big spiritual scene."

The Swami looked up from his beads. "By chanting, everyone will be happy anyway," he said.

"But think of all the good that could come if you—um— *embraced* the dancing," Ginsberg volunteered. "Think of what a unifying spiritual thing that could be."

"Only one thing can unite all men and that is absolute," Lefkowitz said.

" 'And I am lodged in the hearts of all,' " two disciples called cheerfully through the kitchen door.

"Kids who dance can be aware of that, too," Ginsberg said softly.

"You think I'm conservative?" the Swami said. "Tell me." Ginsberg had described the Swami to a reporter from the *Chronicle* as "the Hindu equivalent to a hard-shell Baptist," and the Swami's feelings were hurt.

"Well, for one thing," Ginsberg began, "I really can't see a town like San Francisco full of kids with Brahman strings."

Bhaktivedanta pointed to Lefkowitz and the two kitchen disciples, who had tiptoed over to the rug to listen. "Why not?" he said. "*These* boys are becoming Brahman."

"Hey, is that legal?" Ginsberg asked, laughing.

" 'Bra' means he who has knowledge," the Swami said. "A person who has knowledge believes in God—he is a Brahman."

"It's not birth, it is *destiny*," Lefkowitz said.

"What about American Indians?" Ginsberg asked. "Can you turn American Indians into Brahmans?"

"I can turn anybody into a Brahman," the Swami said. "It is simply a matter of proper training and illumination and of saying 'I am the servant of the servant of the servant of Krishna.'" He added, modestly, that given the time, he could turn San Francisco policemen into sacred-cow protectors, too.

"It's all in the Swami's book—Book One, Chapter Three," Lefkowitz said, jumping up to get a copy from the shelf.

"What about *Rama*krishna?" Ginsberg said. "*He* chanted to Krishna. *He* was the servant of the servant of the servant. What's wrong with him?"

The Swami shook his head. "Ramakrishna chanted? I don't believe it."

Ginsberg told him it was true.

"Well, *that* was good, at least," the Swami said.

"What did he do *bad*?" Ginsberg asked.

"Ramakrishna worshiped Kali!" The Swami shuddered at the thought.

Ginsberg shrugged. "Well, maybe he saw aspects of *Krishna* in Kali," he said.

Bhaktivedanta waved his hands. "Why should he do that?" he asked. "What is it possible to see the same between Krishna and Kali?"

"Perhaps, behind Krishna and Kali, the same reality," Ginsberg said.

Bhaktivedanta reached for his beads. "I accept the *true* shastra," he said.

Ginsberg chuckled. "The Chinese Buddhists call their own shastra a marvelous emptiness," he said.

"Bah," said the Swami. "What is this 'emptiness'?"

Ginsberg slapped him on the knee again. "Swami," he said, "it's probably all just a difference in language and not worth arguing." Then he turned to Lefkowitz. "Like the Swami says, the best thing to do in a case like this is *chant*," he said.

Chapter 6

One day in the winter of 1967, Ginsberg paid a visit to Robert Lowell, who was on his way to the hospital for a rest cure, and Lowell complained to him about having to stop work. He said that the particular hopped-up state of mind in which he found himself was precisely the state of mind in which his best ideas for poetry occurred.

"I told him if he wants to go crazy *normally* and get his work done," Ginsberg remarked later to Orlovsky, "next time I'll invite him to move in here."

After years as the head of a ménage, Ginsberg has come to a state of amused and benevolent *laissez-faire* regarding his domestic arrangements. His apartment, wherever he happens to be living, is usually open to any congenial being who wants to camp there and is willing to help with the cleaning up. Arriving guests are encouraged not to shoot drugs, sell drugs, or freak-out with undue violence on the premises, and then they are directed to a bed, if any beds are available, or a mattress or a piece of floor, advised as to the whereabouts of the instant coffee, the tea bags, the peanut butter and the bathtub cleanser, and afterward left alone. During household orgies they are invited either to participate or to avoid gawking, and although Orlovsky is apt to greet any attractive new arrival with the happy shriek, "Oh, goody, *that's* for Peter!" all preferences in matters of the heart are respected as a family rule.

At home on East Tenth Street, Ginsberg is accustomed to writing to the combined noises of daytime television (Maretta likes soap operas), two stereo speakers (Orlovsky likes raga music), the Uher (his friends like the tapes that Ginsberg makes of his various encounters with policemen), a bombastic telephone, and the steady conversation of scores of habitués. Off and on during the winter of the Human Be-In, five people lived with Ginsberg, Maretta, and the Orlovskys, who were back in the apartment by early February: a hyperthyroid Hindu convert who liked to be called Beelzebub; a young California woodsman with a part-time job in the Eighth Street Bookshop; a teen-age Negro girl from Queens who arrived one night with her suitcase and settled down without a word of explanation to anyone; a friendly amphetamine-head from Tennessee, free on bail at the time, who had refused a deal with a narcotics policeman to set Ginsberg up for a marijuana arrest and who was consequently up for sentencing on several marijuana charges of his own (the policeman himself was arrested a year later—he had made a tidy fortune selling heroin); and, finally, a nubile runaway named Susan, in a state of numbed amorousness, who was particularly attached to Orlovsky at the time. Eventually, all of them moved on and were replaced by other friends. Beelzebub left on a spiritual pilgrimage to Outer Mongolia. The girl from Queens vanished as mysteriously as she had appeared. The boy from

Tennessee broke bail and went to prison. The young woodsman met a charming girl and took a place with her across the street. And Susan was tracked down by a pair of frantic and uncomprehending parents and apparently institutionalized. ("She wasn't much good about the housework anyway," Ginsberg consoled Orlovsky, after she had gone.)

On a more or less typical afternoon at home that winter, Ginsberg was trying to get dressed for a reading in the small and vaguely shipwrecked corner of the apartment that he has reserved as a master bedroom, writer's den, and grand salon. There was snow on the street and on the cars outside, and sunlight, breaking into huge glints, was shooting up through the windows of his old brownstone. Orlovsky had been scrubbing the windows all morning. A pail full of wadded pink Kleenix that he had used —Orlovsky liked the color—was still sitting on the floor, next to the wooden teacher's desk where Ginsberg answers his mail and types up his poems. A white filing cabinet, some old crates, and a big brown bureau, standing in a row by Ginsberg's mattress, were stacked with grocery cartons, books, and papers, two years' worth of Christmas cards, and several pint bottles of Maretta's *friction pour le bain*, and there were pictures of Ginsberg's favorite gods and holy men tacked up on an assortment of doors and walls and bulletin boards. There were also, scattered around the room, an election-meeting notice from the Bolivar-Douglas Reform Democratic Club on Avenue C; a poster from a Fellowship of Reconciliation rally for a visiting Vietnamese monk; a rare Zen flower scroll, to the effect that the absence of life is death, in which the empty spaces formed a skull; a Tibetan silkscreen hanging of the eight terrible defenders of the dharma; some dried flowers in a Coke bottle; Orlovsky's workout weights; a gift basket of d'Anjou pears from Charles and Company on upper Madison Avenue; a "Fuck for Peace" banner; a crayon drawing by one of the children of Ginsberg's Puerto Rican neighbors; a tambourine; an etching called *"La Danse Divine des Derviches"*; an invitation to a "multi-media vigil" for the Vietnamese; a copy of the *Salutation to the Triple Gem*, phonetically transliterated from the Sino-Japanese; a postcard from Jacques Barzun; and the family collection of slogan buttons, amulets, and beads.

Ginsberg had just been straightening up—plumping some cushions on the floor and pulling an old Army blanket up over the sheets and pillow on his mattress, and now he was in the process of extricating his socks from the bottom of a pile involving an alarm clock, a roll of toilet paper, a box of saltine crackers, and a few pear cores. Sitting at the desk, watching Ginsberg closely, was a man by the name of Carl Solomon, Ginsberg's old friend from the Columbia Psychiatric Institute and the mad holy hero of the poem "Howl." Ginsberg once referred to Solomon as an "advanced CCNY Dadaist intellectual." He said that Solomon, in fact, had presented himself at the Institute, demanding a lobotomy, because as a worthy disciple of Artaud he had wanted to make a sort of Dada gesture-in-the-absolute. Solomon was now a respectable publisher's reader at Ace Books; and today he was dressed accordingly, in a somber blue suit and a plain gray tie. His large round face was nicked in several places from a particularly close shave.

Ginsberg stopped straightening to say that his friend looked a little edgy. Solomon, who had just published a book of reflections on his madhouse days called *Mishaps Perhaps*, was going to read with Ginsberg at New Jersey State that night.

Solomon shook his head. "Lately I have been amusing myself pretending to be on shows with David Susskind and Joe Pyne," he said. "It keeps me up nights."

"Groovy," Ginsberg said, picking up his brown-tweed jacket from the floor and walking over to the bureau to select the appropriate beads. "How do you make out?"

"Well, yesterday I presented myself to Susskind as someone

who had actually marched in a May Day parade," Solomon replied. In a moment he added, "It was 1946, to be exact."

"Did Susskind take it seriously?" Ginsberg asked him.

"He must have—I sounded so anguished about it," Solomon said.

Just then a tall and rather wild-eyed man in a bright red jacket came sprinting into Ginsberg's room.

"Am I out of breath!" the man panted. He was a local poet by the name of Ray Bremser.

Ginsberg told him to calm down.

"Like, it's my anniversary, man," Bremser said.

"Blessings," Ginsberg said. He had dropped to his hands and knees and was groping under a cushion for his left shoe.

Bremser spun around. "Hey, you're getting fat, Carl."

"I'm doing all right," Solomon said. "Did you read my book? I read *your* book."

"Naw, I've got a *new* book coming out," Bremser said. "*Two* printers so far have refused to print it."

"Was it obscene?" Solomon said.

Bremser sat down on one of Maretta's suitcases, which was in service as a chair, to think. "They told me it was," he said. "It had words that they say are obscene."

"That's awful," Solomon said.

"I wrote it in *one* night—in the can, in solitary confinement," Bremser went on over the din of a telephone which was ringing in the next room. "But it was a beautiful, gentle book, I don't give a fuck what *anybody* says."

A door by the desk opened and Orlovsky poked out his head. He was dressed in some sort of gleaming black jockstrap. Solomon stared at him, disapproving.

"It's some young artist on the phone," Orlovsky whispered. "He wants to use the camper to take some paintings somewhere."

Ginsberg shrugged. "It's up to you," he said.

"Well, it's *your* truck," Orlovsky whispered.

"Think of it as *your* truck," Ginsberg said.

Orlovsky came back into the room. He began prowling around the room, turning over boxes and opening drawers. "Where's Maretta?" he said finally.

Ginsberg, who was at the window now, sorting through a stack of poems for the reading, told him that Maretta and Beelzebub had gone to southern New Jersey to inspect a fledgling Tibetan monastery and size up some of the incarnate lamas there.

"You know something," Bremser said, seizing Orlovsky by the arm, "the *East Village Other* is going to do a story on me—on all those printers who refuse to print my books."

"You know who has the best titles for books?" Solomon mused. "Anais Nin."

"So I need money, man," Bremser said, while Ginsberg padded toward them, looking for some place to spread out his poems. "Like, it's my *anniversary*. I better take the wench to dinner. Right? And maybe a movie, if the meal's cheap."

"Isn't that nice, Ginzy, it's his anniversary," Orlovsky crooned. He reached into Ginsberg's pocket and began pulling out dollar bills.

"Ten all right?" Ginsberg said.

Bremser collapsed on the mattress, apparently overcome.

"Julius is lost," Orlovsky remarked.

Solomon jumped up. "Julius is lost? You're not worried?"

"The best thing, love, is not to worry," Orlovsky said. He looked especially authoritative, twirling a strand of pubic hair much as a professor, between significant pronouncements, might twirl a mustache. Ginsberg began to laugh.

"Maybe some nice middle-aged woman has him," Solomon volunteered.

Orlovsky nodded happily and tiptoed away. A few minutes later he was singing and splashing in the bathtub, and two more visitors were in Ginsberg's room, rifling through the d'Anjou pears. One of them was a teaching assistant in English at one of the state universities. His name was Allen Tobias, and he had dropped in, he said, to do a little work on his Ginsberg bibliography. The other visitor was a boy named Bobby.

"Gregory about?" Bobby asked, pointing down the hall to a closed door.

Ginsberg nodded.

"Aha, so it's Corso in there," Bremser shouted. "I knew it was *somebody*."

"Do you really suppose that Gregory is Gilgamesh?" Solomon asked them. Bremser shook his head, but Bobby shrugged. Corso, who had just moved into the top of a bunk bed in Julius' room, had spent the past three years closeted in a cabin in Crete, reading Sumerian epics, and at the moment—much to the amusement of Beelzebub—he was of the opinion that his proper name was Gilgamesh.

"I don't know," Bobby said. "Like, I don't pry into people's private lives." He began licking a particularly juicy pear.

"I don't think he's Gilgamesh," Solomon said.

Ginsberg was now trying to organize his papers on a small spare patch of floor. When the phone rang again, Solomon reached for it.

"A young lady wishes to speak to Peter," Solomon said.

"Oh, that's *too* good—it's for Peter," Orlovsky shrieked with pleasure from the depths of the bathtub. He came skipping into the room, shedding soapsuds, and after banging on his ear a couple of times he grabbed the telephone.

"Peter speaking," he sang. "I'm in the bathtub. Gotta get back in, sweetie. Right-o. About midnight. *Adios*." Then he turned to Solomon. "Lovely girl," he said.

"Peter's ability is *verbal*," Solomon told Ginsberg after Orlovsky had gone. "I took an aptitude test the other day, and they said that most of *my* ability was verbal, too. They said I should consider social work."

"The bureaucracy—work in that," Ginsberg said, laughing. "Or work in the CIA. *Ramparts* says everybody works for the CIA. All those Congress for Cultural Freedom cats." Ginsberg thought for a minute. "Yeah," he said. "Apply to the CIA, Carl. I figure they want red-blooded, healthy Americans—I might even apply, too."

"No, the aptitude test said that I had the same interests as people successful in literature, not spying," Solomon said. And he added, to Tobias, "I don't have the same interests as Ginsberg, though. I get called a beatnik sometime. Do I *look* like one?"

Tobias shook his head.

"What's your sign, Carl?" a gravelly voice demanded from somewhere behind them. The voice belonged to Corso, who was standing, yawning, at the bedroom door. Corso had been spending the day in bed, and his bright black hair—Corso loved his hair and was said to put in a good deal of time examining it, under a magnifying mirror, for signs of encroaching baldness— was sticking up on end like a stiff mop. There was a particularly glowering expression on his face, due in part to disposition and in part to the fact that his two front teeth had departed from his mouth one day in Crete, under sudden and mysterious circumstances. Even Bremser shuddered a little as Corso strolled into the room, scratching at his chest and still yawning. He had on a pair of baggy tan corduroys, and he was evidently looking for one of Ginsberg's shirts. Ginsberg gestured toward the brown bureau.

"I'm an Aries," Solomon said.

"So am I," Corso said. "I'm told, 'Beware of Scorpios.' "

"I myself am opposed to anybody telling me what to do," Solomon said. He was interrupted by another knock, which was followed by the appearance of a young man of about fifteen, bundled up in a sheepskin overcoat. The young man walked around slowly, taking in everything. He had found Ginsberg's address in the telephone book, he said, and had decided to drop by after school and introduce himself. Ginsberg offered him a pear.

"Will you sign my book?" the boy asked Ginsberg, pulling a

fat schoolbook out of the pocket of his overcoat. It was called *Civilization*, a title which amused Ginsberg and inspired Corso to begin talking about the contributions of Sumerians. Ginsberg, Bremser, Solomon, and Corso signed the book.

"Boy, kid, you could sell it for twenty bucks now," Corso remarked.

The boy sat down.

Ginsberg headed for the front door, with his stack of poetry under his arm. "I guess I better do this in the car, going over," Ginsberg said.

Ginsberg sometimes complains that his household could stand the respectable, steadying influence of a mother-father-baby-in residence. He tells everyone that he wants to have children, and in California he consulted the *I Ching* on the advisability of starting a family with Maretta. According to Snyder, who cast the *I Ching* for Ginsberg and interpreted its forecast, "The weather was generally favorable, but there were a few disturbing winds." Maretta took this as a sign that she was not yet spiritually ready for housekeeping, and in May of 1967 she left for Mongolia herself, to pay her respects at what she had heard was "a really far-out lamasary."

"The difficulties that nuts and poets and visionaries and seekers like Maretta have," Ginsberg remarked after Maretta went away, "are often the same kind of difficulties people have from LSD. The social disgrace—*dis*grace—attached to certain states of soul. The confrontation with a society—or a family, for that matter—which is going in a different direction, and the ineptness of the initiate, who is totally dependent during those confrontations on the blissful will of others, at knowing how to handle his perception without becoming fearful or blowing his cool. Knowing how to feel human and holy and not like a madman in a world which is rigid and materialistic and all caught up in the immediate necessities. Like if it's time to cook supper and you're busy communing, the world says there must be something wrong with you. Or like, after my Blake vision, when I tried to evoke the sensations of the experience myself, artificially, by dancing around my apartment chanting a sort of homemade mantra: 'Come, spirit. O spirit, spirit, come. Come, spirit. O spirit, spirit, come.' Something like that. There I was, in the dark, in an apartment in the middle of Harlem, whirling like a dervish and invoking powers. And everybody I tried to talk to about it thought I was crazy. Not just that psychiatrist. The two girls who lived next door. My father. My teachers. Even most of my friends. Now, in a society which was open and dedicated to spirit, like in India, my actions and my address would have been considered quite normal. Had I been transported to a street-corner potato-curry shop in Benares and begun acting that way, I would have been seen as in some special, holy sort of state and sent on my way to the burning grounds, to sit and meditate. And when I got home, I would have been like gently encouraged to express myself, to work it out, and then left alone. I would have been understood."

Ginsberg's auditory encounter with William Blake was what he calls a "natural vision"—that is, a vision that occurs spontaneously, without inducement or drugs. It began, according to his many accounts of it, late one afternoon in the summer of 1948, when Ginsberg, who was lying on his bed reading "Ah! Sun-Flower" from Blake's *Songs of Experience*, suddenly heard the poem "speak itself" in a grave, oracular voice, which he took to be the voice of the Master. It continued through "The Sick Rose," "A Little Girl Lost," and "Hear the Voice of the Bard! who Present, Past & Future, Sees," accompanied, Ginsberg says, by intense religious illumination. "The thing I felt was that there was this big god over all, who was completely aware and completely conscious of everybody and at the same time completely the same as everybody, and that the whole purpose of being born was to wake up to Him," Ginsberg says. "I felt everything vibrating in one harmony—all past efforts and desires, all present realizations. The workmen, fifty years ago, chiseling the cornice of the building across the street from me, the sun laboring to produce blackness. Everything was vibrating toward this one instant of consciousness. And I realized all this, just as I imagine that somebody having a baby realizes in retrospect that all love-making—starting with the gazes and hand-holdings and masturbations and childhood dates and going to the movies—tended toward birth. And I felt that even *my* previous ponderings had been harmoniously flower-petaled toward this final understanding of what it was all about and that all my poetic musings about supreme reality were prophetic, really, and just the sweet, well-intentioned strivings of a poor mind to reach what was already there."

PART II

My desire to share, not MONOPOLIZE the images,
because I don't want to be ALONE on Earth
                    —from a poem, "To the Hell's Angels,"
                    by Allen Ginsberg

Chapter 1

On a sunny California morning in the middle of that faraway winter term of 1967, word spread through the Berkeley Student Union that Allen Ginsberg was about to hold office hours in the cafeteria upstairs. Ginsberg, who had come to Berkeley for the week as a sort of roving guest professor of poetry and miscellaneous visionary information, had just been spotted at the cafeteria counter, purchasing a large number of hamburgers, and, as it had been reported, at the moment he was in the process of setting up headquarters at a big round table in the middle of the adjoining patio. Most of the students who were stopping at the cafeteria between classes for coffee and doughnuts, recognized Ginsberg as he raced around from table to table, borrowing chairs. He had become a familiar sight on the campus since his famous flower-power speech in the fall of 1965, and by now everybody there had heard at least one version of the saga of Ginsberg and the Berkeley Vietnam Day march. Ginsberg had written his instructions—"How To Make a March/Spectacle"—for exemplary Berkeley demonstrations after the Oakland police force turned back an earlier peace march, en route to the Oakland Army Terminal, at the border of the two cities, and the local Hell's Angels, who happened to be lurking behind the police barricades, took the opportunity to attack the demonstrators with an alarming assortment of chains, knives, and clubs. The rally at which he read them, a few weeks later, was understandably gloomy. Some of the students wanted to arm themselves against the Angels, but Ginsberg, at the rally, made it clear that he was determined to *love* the Angels, if not into outright friendliness, at least into a temporary state of truce. He knew some of them from parties at the La Honda hideaway of his friend Ken Kesey, and he was naturally disappointed when his first appeals, including a rally poem with the memorably accurate lines "BUT NOBODY WANTS TO REJECT THE SOULS OF THE HELL'S ANGELS/or make them change—/WE JUST DON'T WANT TO GET BEAT UP," failed to move the motorcycle outlaws, who replied by issuing bulletins to the effect that they would get the students next time. A withdrawal would be unmanly, they confided to Ginsberg, and it would wreck their publicity. The students, for their part, began to suspect that the Angels had the blessings of the Oakland Citizens Aroused, a group of self-appointed right-wing vigilantes, not to mention most of the local police. Negotiations between the pacifists and the motorcyclists, which had begun after the rally, quickly broke down. Then, with a "make-up" peace march less than a week away, Ginsberg arrived at the home of Ralph (Sonny) Barger, the president of the Oakland Angels, armed with a pocketful of LSD and his battered text of the *Prajna Paramita Sutra* and accompanied by Kesey and the Merry Pranksters, Kesey's friends. Barger, who was probably armed too, was accompanied by his largest, strongest men. The reports of what went on that night are by now apocryphal, but the participants seem to agree that the meeting ended near dawn with several highly ecstatic Angels chanting the wisdom of the Bodhisattva in Sino-Japanese. One of Barger's lieutenants who was there told a reporter that Ginsberg had been "otherworldly." "For a guy that ain't straight at all," the Angel apparently said, "he's the straightest sonofabitch I've ever seen. Man, you shoulda been there when he told Sonny he loved him . . . Sonny didn't know *what* the hell to say." On the afternoon before the march, Barger called a press conference and solemnly handed out a short mimeographed release: "Although we have stated our intention to counter-demonstrate at this despicable, un-American activity, we believe that in the interest of public safety and the protection of the good name of Oakland, we would not justify the VDC [Vietnam Day Committee] by our presence . . . because our patriotic concern for what these people are doing to a great nation may provoke us into violent acts . . ."

Ever since the march, which turned out to be a flowery and indeed exemplary spectacle, Ginsberg made a point of stopping at Berkeley whenever an opportunity occurred. Last night, when he read at the Student Union, some four thousand students had jammed the auditorium to hear his chantings and his latest poems. "Flower Power" buttons and the "Jewish Power" bagel buttons that had been restocked in quantity by the local button emporiums in honor of the poet's visit, were in evidence on every second coat and poncho, and today there were still a few "Allen Ginsberg for President" signs, left over from the reading, propped against the patio walls. Ginsberg, noticing them, grinned. His big toothy smile, together with his whiskers and his round glasses, gave him the look of a hairy, happy, somewhat avuncular owl. Ginsberg, in fact, had just told the cafeteria cook who fixed his hamburgers that he was particularly happy in his new professorial incarnation. He had worked for half an hour after breakfast polishing his hiking shoes, and then he had put on a rumpled, baggy, but otherwise impeccable dark gray suit, which he had bought at Brooks Brothers for testifying at the subcommittee hearing on LSD. For decoration, he had chosen the bright flowered tie out of his bag of presents from the San Francisco Gathering of the Tribes for a Human Be-In, in January; an Indian shell necklace made by the grandmother of a Santo Domingo Pueblo he had met in the Haight-Ashbury; and a lead Tibetan dorje, which, according to lamaic researches, is either a sacred thunderbolt in the shape of a sacred phallus or a sacred phallus in the shape of a sacred thunderbolt. Finally, just before leaving Divisidero Street, where he was still staying, he stood at the bathroom mirror over a sink full of water and carefully plastered down his hair. Orlovsky and Maretta, who drove over to Berkeley with Ginsberg in the family Volkswagen camper, had checked him out for flaws at the Bay Bridge.

At the moment, Orlovsky was scrubbing down the cafeteria counter where he and Maretta were waiting in line for tea. Ginsberg, having collected six blue patio chairs, had just sat down outside to his professional duties. Three students were already at the table, talking about the reading, and a fourth young man, who had been circling the table hesitantly with an orange in his hand and a paperback Spinoza under his arm, was in the process of asking Ginsberg to share the orange with him.

Ginsberg burst out laughing. "For the love of God, why didn't you just *say* so?" Ginsberg said, nodding toward an empty chair. "I was beginning to think you were some kind of mad super-spy from Ronald Reagan's office, prowling around like that."

"Peace," the boy said. He turned over half of his orange and accepted a hamburger in return.

"*Om*," Ginsberg replied. "Were *you* at the reading too?"

The boy had been studying. He said that he was sorry. "I was at the Be-In, though," he volunteered. "It was beautiful."

"Naw, it didn't make it," one of the other boys announced. He was a drama major and he had dressed up for classes in a new motorcycle jacket and a violently flowered blouse. "Too many kids wandering around zonked out."

Orlovsky, who had arrived with a tray of tea and cornflakes, peered at the boy with a frenetically tender look that made Ginsberg laugh. "Did you extend your hand?" Orlovsky said. "You gotta extend your hand." Orlovsky seized the boy's hand and wiped it with his rag. The boy blushed.

Maretta, who had just finished a hamburger, thereby breaking a ban on meat that she had been observing during the full moon, looked him over appraisingly.

"The trouble was the people were looking, not *being*," he said.

Ginsberg shrugged. "Well, there were plenty of pretty things to see," he said. "Things like *that*." Ginsberg pointed to the striped serape, at the next table, that was covered with buttons reading "Impeach Reagan," "I Am a Human Being," "Pot," "Strike for Anything," and "Sterilize LBJ."

The boy in the serape pulled his chair over immediately. "I saw in the *Daily Cal* that you were going to hold office hours *all* week," he said. "Boy, it blew my mind."

Ginsberg thanked him.

Orlovsky skipped off with the empty tray and seemed to be looking for something to clean. He had tied his long brown hair into a pony tail with a red shoelace, and it was flying straight out into the wind as he careened around the crowded patio, arms and legs at odds, bumping into people and leading with his tray into deep, apologetic bows. Ginsberg, watching him, looked amused.

"Is he in a—a normal state?" the boy in the serape asked, staring at Orlovsky, who was grabbing dirty dishes off tables.

"He's a vegetarian, and it gives him goofy kicks," Ginsberg said. "Like once we had to go to court for some parking ticket or something. Peter came leaping in, kind of the way he is now. The judge looked at him and said 'Five bucks,' but Peter said, 'The windows in here are dirty, take ten.' "

"You're really *living* with him?" the boy said.

Ginsberg grinned. "In terms of tenderness and understanding, we're probably doing better than a lot of your parents are," he said. "Anyway, I've got a girl now"—Ginsberg nodded at Maretta, who was staring at a crystal bead—"and so it's all working out naturally. It's probably just like any other long marriage. Like, it's not a question of sex any more—we just pass the time together."

The boy in the serape fiddled philosophically with his budding John Lennon mustache.

"Like, I'm not an advocate of homosexuality," Ginsberg went on, "but everybody's got their bag, and those bags are not that bad."

"What did *you* think of the Be-In, Allen?" the boy with the orange broke in.

Ginsberg thought for a minute. "Groovy," he said finally. "I thought it was groovy, but I wish it had been more political."

' "More of a—a *manifestation*, like the Vietnam Day marches," the boy with the orange agreed.

"Man, you make politics and love seem compatible," the drama major said. "That's not where politics is at."

"Why not?" Ginsberg asked him. "Even a show of this many faces at a table is political, in the strict sense."

"That's not what the hippies would tell you," the boy said.

Ginsberg laughed and told the students that they looked like hippies themselves.

The boy with the orange said no—they were activists. "As I see it, from an activist point of view," he said, "the hippies haven't taken a Bodhisattva vow to return from Nirvana and organize a heavenly community."

"Put it this way," Ginsberg said. "The hippies—that is, the psychedelics—have got the consciousness all right, but they have the problem of how to manifest it in the community without risking the pitfalls of a Fascist organization. You people—the radicals—have a real vision of the material and social ills of the society, but you've got pretty much the same problem. The hippies have deeper insight into consciousness, the radicals more information about the workings and the nature of consciousness in the world." Ginsberg eyed the boy in the serape and the boy with the orange. "So like it would be really groovy to see a meeting going on between people like you two and, say, Mario Savio from here and some of the leaders from the Haight, like Allen Cohen, who runs the *Oracle*, or a guy named Mike Bowen, who's going to start an indigenous psychedelic ashram," Ginsberg said. "It could be like allied seekers getting together."

"Goddam right," the boy with the orange said, but a boy at the next table—evidently anti-hippie—leaned over and muttered that hippies were in a "totalitarian bag." He said that in his opinion hippies were good for nothing but drooling and stringing beads.

Maretta looked at him.

"Listen," Ginsberg said, laughing, "don't be so defensive. Sure, they're a little fuzzy, but they're not putting *you* down by making beads."

"Yeah, but they're putting us down for doing anything else," the boy said. "Like, we have a peace march and *they* turn up all upset, saying that marching's not dropping-out, marching's a bad bag, marching's not *pure*."

Ginsberg shrugged and told the boy that he was probably right. "But they're still on to something," he said. "They're committed to a community of awareness, to control of anger, to all mammals"—Ginsberg chuckled and said that he liked the word mammals—"to the preservation of the planet, to art, to tolerance, to sexuality as a mode of social communication, to the entire body rather than just that part called the cerebral cortex"—he rapped the boy in the serape gently on the head—"to the clarification of the earth's atmosphere, to a new realization of human experience without fear, to an end to bullshit." Ginsberg threw up his hands. "So you're going to write them off because they like to make *beads*?"

"Why don't *they* say those things?" the boy with the orange said.

"Oh, come on," Ginsberg said. "Because they're *inarticulate*.

And anyway, why blame the hippies for everything? What about the political specialists? Have they come up with a blueprint? How can you ask the hippies to come up with a blueprint for political neighborly action when no one else has? As it is, they have a more viable community than anyone else. And as far as you people go, it's necessary for both groups to get together for any political action to be possible at all. Any conflict between students and hippies would be sheer egomania."

Ginsberg stopped talking to wave over a chubby blond boy in gray pants and a plain short-sleeved shirt who had been standing a few feet off from the table, trying to catch his eye. The boy was a reporter for one of the campus papers. He had interviewed Ginsberg earlier that morning, and he had been thinking a lot, he said, about what Ginsberg had told him about LSD. The reporter looked around at the other students. He seemed a little embarrassed to be asking about drugs in such psychedelically bedecked and flowered company.

"Look," Ginsberg said quietly when the reporter had dragged over a chair. "You were a little nervous about LSD, right?"

"Oh, man, why?" the boy in the serape said.

The reporter gulped, but he nodded earnestly.

"Well, *my thing*," Ginsberg went on, "is that meditation can lead to the same patience and awareness and illumination as LSD. To, like, the vision of acid but *without* acid. Dig?"

The boy replied bravely that it was his journalistic duty to experiment.

"Man, if you take acid, have some hash around," Maretta announced, looking up from a copy of *Newsweek* on the table. She had been admiring a picture of herself in a spread on the Human Be-In, and she passed it over for the reporter to see. Maretta looked approximately the same today. The reporter, who seemed to be having trouble finding something appropriate to say to her, finally told Maretta that the picture was very inspiring. She smiled wanly. Then she said she would describe her own last trip for him. Maretta had taken LSD the week before at a log cabin in Big Sur, which she, Ginsberg, Snyder, and Orlovsky had borrowed from the Ferlinghettis for a short vacation in the woods. Ginsberg had thought about taking some too—he wanted to make a tape of his reactions—but he had decided against it when it started raining early on the appointed morning, explaining to his friends that the sky looked "too uncongenial" for a good trip. Maretta, who was undeterred by the rain, had walked off into the woods alone to inspect wet leaves under her crystal bead. Ginsberg and Snyder stayed home, working on a first line for a colloquial and chant-worthy translation of the *Prajna Paramita Sutra*. Orlovsky made fudge.

Maretta sighed slightly after her story, and then withdrew into herself. Ginsberg told the reporter that she was "a wise dakini from Boston and Tibet," who liked to think about things.

The reporter was impressed.

"Look," Ginsberg said. "You be careful. Like, if you're going to take acid, make sure you have competent friends around. And a lot of nature. A lot of familiar, reassuring images to focus on—like your favorite gods, mandalas—"

"Then you pick out *any* mandala, any one that appeals to you?" the reporter asked.

"What else?" Ginsberg shrugged. "Let some psychotic shithead pick out a big ugly symbol for you and then have a bad trip?"

Ginsberg had linked his fingers into a curious and rather alarming configuration, which he told the reporter was a good mudra to learn for expelling demons. He said that precisely this mudra had come in handy on Divisidero Street just the other morning, when a couple of local hoods had grabbed his marketing bag.

"They got my eggs," Ginsberg said, "but when I attacked with the mudra they dropped the bag and ran like they had seen some crazy monster."

The boy with the orange tapped him on the shoulder. "Allen,

I don't want to interrupt or anything," he said, "but what did you mean a while ago about hippies having a new kind of human experience?"

"I was talking about a mutation of the race," Ginsberg replied, tipping back in his blue patio chair.

"I know *that*, but I still don't know what you *meant*," the boy with the orange said.

"What I meant," Ginsberg said, "is that the past is bunk for people now. All past consciousness is bunk. History is bunk. Like Henry Ford said about technology—there's nothing to be learned from history any more. We're in science fiction now. All the revolutions and the old methods and techniques for changing consciousness are bankrupt. We're back to magic, to psychic life. Like the civil rights movement hasn't succeeded in altering the fear-consciousness of the white Southern middle class, but the hippies might."

"But the civil rights movement's got power," the boy with the orange said. "The hippies, they haven't got any power."

Ginsberg groaned. "Don't you know that power's a hallucination?" he said. "The civil rights movement, Sheriff Rainey, *Time Magazine*, McNamara, Mao—it's all a hallucination. No one can get away with saying that's real. All public reality's a script, and anybody can write the script the way he wants. The warfare's psychic now. Whoever controls the language, the images, controls the race. Power all boils down to whether McNamara gets up on the right side of the bed. And who's McNamara anyway? He's a lot of TV dots. *That's* public reality. Like imagine what would happen if McNamara got on television and started saying, 'Some of the fellows, some of the human beings we've been fighting with' instead of 'some of the Communists.' Words like 'Communist,' 'capitalist'—they're language as hypnosis, as an outrage against feeling. They're not the reality we know in the bedroom; they're comic-strip reality. They ought to be printed in the papers in those little balloons."

"Yeah, man, but that's life, that's where it's at," the boy from the drama department remarked, helping himself to the remainder of Orlovsky's cornflakes.

"Look, do you want to roll back the darkness or sit there complaining?" Ginsberg said. He told the boy to start writing letters about reality to the public people. *He* had been writing letters like that when *he* was in college, he said. Harry Truman had got quite a few of them then. And last year, after the Berkeley peace march, he had even been moved to sit down and try communicating with Robert McNamara. His letter read:

Dear Mr. McNamara, I am not sure you will respect my advice, but anyway, you cannot help but be interested if I can reach you with this message, so let us try.

The first thing is, be calm, there is no essential threat to anybody's ultimate being. Not yours, you also are safe, as is one supposed to be your or our enemy. He is also safe.

The reason for this is, as the old Chinese sages recognized earlier in time, that the very flesh universe we find ourselves trapped in is, in its nature, unthreatening because it is empty—illusory—Shakespeare & the Chinese agree—Prospero the Wise Man agrees—everything's all right because we are inhabiting a very special realm of pure Dream.

But as I get excited as Mao Tse-tung (whoever he is) gets frightened, as you take things so seriously, the dream turns to a kind of physical nightmare, with apparent conflict and—ugh—suffering death—well, death is built into it in any case—but the anxiety and paranoia—fear of a cosmic ENEMY is the stricken-feeling anxiety chord that runs thru

Everybody's heart in America right now tonight—and in Vietnam or China we can only imagine &—try to calm that panic.

Now, are you doing things to calm that panic, or are you now, generally in fantasy or manifest thought (orders for more bomb), seized by that panic and acting it out? and so creating material conditions for it (the panic-fear-paranoia of Invasion by alien forces from some Outside) to flourish in everybody's mind—our own mind as well as the minds of China?

I do not know directly personally from contact with you what your subjective attitude is, but from what I read in the reduplicated Images of the mass media, you yourself are sending out waves of anxiety and fear.

Now given your material prominence and TV centrality and known and unknown governmental power-centralization, you must realize that it is your Will, your Fantasy, that dominates the mind-screen images of vast—not all—regions of the populace.

But there are large regions of age and youth whose conciousness operates independently of the sense of fear you manifest. If not fear, the sense of conflict.

A question of staying calm, sitting in the room, the war will end, nobody ultimately wants it, a small area of consciousness living in fear of the shattering of its own Imagery—may prefer that & pain & death to realization—that the war does not actually exist, except in your mind and the mind of your coresponding Powers on the "Other Side."

Both sides are an illusion—you must by now have read basic Buddhist or Bob Dylan heard, texts & advices how to escape from the trap.

Unfortunately both you and Johnson—seem to me—surrounded by men who have not actually controlled their own Passions—simply, angryness, tendencies toward self-righteous exclusion of other forms of consciousness. The waves of emotional hysteria—both sides—not any material struggle for space in the universe—are the problem. In Other words the cold war all along has been an Emotional problem of those panicked by power and leadership—they have not been calm & tranquil— They—and you—have separated yourself out, away, from the Communists and other life forms, and have not made sufficient effort to provide conditions for these life forms to "co."—Yes —"exist." Coexistence—unless you anticipate a Wagnerian battle for control of the Universe—Dualities and ultimate conflict—do you dream of such a thing necessary—many do. Many posit their whole consciousness on early fear that it's kill or be devoured— Anyway—Coexistence is the only mode of consciousness which will allow space for both you and the Chinese to exist on the planet. Unless that space is provided and made way for, paid for with cooperation and COMMUNICATION on basic psychic levels—reassurance, etc., such as I am giving you now—has to be given the Chinese—Unless as I say that is given—a straight two-handed calm show of amiability—

free joy even—Naturally the Chinese are going to feel persecuted and paranoid. And if they feel that—in response to what is basically the Ill-Will of Americans toward their supposed Threat —then they will act unstable and hostile and we—beginning with what was a fixed white Image, and an artificial Moral image—superiority—will also act hostile.

So we have two life forms—both brothers in their desire for life, both trapped in the dream that it is somehow "Real," both in separate universes of mental suspicion.

Naturally you'll have a conflict that way.

If you can find the imagination to break thru that—even if it involves the bankruptcy of your whole phenomenal Purpose, your whole concluded idea system, your SELF and its apparent sensory impressions—yea yea yes—we & you too share in the madness, you are not more Sane than my appeal to you after all, dear—I mean with your vast Armada you're going to think I'm unbalanced or don't understand the pith experience of the TRAP? Well, we're all desperate, myself the most, so certainly you'll suffer no more in change than me, or Mao Tse-tung—

But the change must begin inside you, not Outside.

I have specific suggestions how to manifest this change—but it would mean a healthy change for America, and China, and be happy and not frightened to see you and talk to you or anyone else you think hath focal Hand in the balances of phantasy & thought.

No war is necessary, it never was outside of our fear contaminating the Chinese and their fear contaminating us—it's all hysteria—only solution is literally to cut thru the hysteria to a ground—our own natural lucidity and wrinkled eyes and flesh feel—where we can all exist together, such as this strange existence is, without the tremor and tightening of body and fantasy agitation of mind—into uncontrolled isolation-fear and wrath army consequent.

That's where "it all is," no place else, neither in a preordained dialectic or some logical imperative of "History."

Poets now say History is over; what they mean is that the reality approaching and the possible Doom or liberation from encroaching serpent-fear is a purely subjective matter. It's already time for you, & Leaders, to take on that subjective responsibility and not set it outside yourself. I'm taking it on by writing you this letter and offering you my Self to come and if need be calm your fear that anyone need be "conquered" any more.

Please reply if you have read and understood this with your own eyes. Thank you,

Allen Ginsberg

"So we've got our story and out there they've got their story," the boy from the drama department said when Ginsberg was through talking about the letter to McNamara. "So why fight it, man? Like what does it matter?"

"Well, *fuck you*, you just don't want to work," Ginsberg yelled. "That's the trouble with the hippies. If they'd get out and work, they'd have the psychic power to deal with that kind of public insanity."

"So what can *we* do, Allen?" the boy with the orange said.

"You cats can like trust your own *personal* reality, trust your visionary responses and your sexual responses," Ginsberg said. "Be kind. Control your anger. Understand who's using the illusion of language. Chip in ten bucks each and hire a lawyer for when one of you gets busted. Register and vote."

"You mean like history and power are a whim?" the boy in the serape interrupted, looking delighted. "That's groovy!"

"Man, what's all this whim thing?" the drama major grumbled. "*Whim?* Vietnam's a whim?"

"Precisely a whim," Ginsberg said, laughing.

"That's power, man," the boy said. "And anyway, it's not so easy to change people's whims."

"Hell, no, it's easier than anything," Ginsberg broke in. "Ever been in a madhouse? I have."

The reporter looked up from the notes that he was making on how to prepare for his LSD trip. "Do you really think they're crazy?" he asked Ginsberg. "I mean, the people who run the war? Do you really think they really don't know what they're doing?"

"How would *you* explain it?" Ginsberg said.

"Hey, I know what we should all do," the boy in the serape said suddenly. "Start preaching 'Down with whimsy!' Run around with big 'Down with whimsy' signs. That'd be beautiful."

"How about 'Make war not love' or 'War is character building,' " Ginsberg suggested.

"Say, maybe I should take yage instead of LSD," the reporter said. He had just entered a new heading in his notebook: "Sacred Vines."

"It's all the same," Ginsberg replied. "Just a shorter trip, that's all." He sounded weary. "Anyhow, I don't know why you keep on *insisting* that you have to take something. You know, if you've got things to do, drugs can be like very *inconvenient*."

"A shorter trip," the reporter repeated, shaking his head. "That sounds great."

"Yage can make you vomit," Ginsberg volunteered.

Maretta poked the reporter with her crystal bead. "I took DMT once," she said. "I had a fucking trip. Visions. Very intense." Then she paused thoughtfully and added that she had had a bad headache for the next two days. The reporter wrote down "Dimethyltryptamine" and put "headache" next to it.

Ginsberg stood up and stretched. He had a class to teach in an hour, he said, and he had promised to give Peter Collier, a writer from *Ramparts* Sunday paper, some time before then. Collier, who had been circling the patio for half an hour, moved toward Ginsberg when he stretched. He waited until Ginsberg found Orlovsky—Orlovsky turned up at the other end of the patio, still clearing dishes, to the helpless astonishment of a dozen busboys—and then he motioned Ginsberg to a quiet table inside the cafeteria.

"I'm an ambassador from Squaresville," Collier began, flicking open his pad and leaning forward in a professional, confidential way.

Ginsberg looked at him. "Why categorize yourself?" he said.

"Well, I'm from *Ramparts*," Collier said.

"What are you trying to do, pull rank?" Ginsberg asked him. "So *you're* from *Ramparts*. *I'm* teaching at U.C." Then he frowned. "We're *all* in the same boat," he said.

Chapter 2

At a time when the students who reign on campuses as awesome and intractable radicals are coolly regarded by their own dropped-out contemporaries as unregenerate conformists to a national school-and-success syndrome, Ginsberg, reading and teaching at colleges, has been one of the very few links between the classroom and the communal pad. He is a funny, eloquent teacher, and an admitted ham. As a reader, he is by rapid turns rapturous, weepy, plaintive, outraged, comical, heartbreaking, and then rapturous again. After a preliminary puff of marijuana or a few minutes of chanting or yogic breathing exercises, he is also capable of making booming oracular pronouncements out of whatever jottings he happens to have around. By now, Ginsberg has put in the better part of three years on the college circuit. Most of his recent work is still waiting to be typed, spread out in sections over dozens of School Time composition books and on the long tapes that he records in cars, trains, diners, and motel rooms as he zigzags back and forth across the country on his tours. The possibilities of "dictated poetry," with its unedited rhythms, its impressionistic flow, and the immediacy of its digressions, interruptions, roughnesses, and background noises, have always interested Ginsberg, but lately he has had little or no chance to write poems any other way. He likes to complain about the frantic life he leads. He says that sometimes, in the middle of a reading, he longs for the simple, private pleasures of a homey Hindu kirtan or a sacred orgy among friends, and he talks about escaping to the woods to write for a year or two. But this is a move that he has always managed to postpone. His own sadhana is as a public man, and, offered an option out, he inevitably ignores it and moves on.

In the fall of 1965, when a Guggenheim Poetry Fellowship gave Ginsberg six thousand dollars and a free hand in spending it, he bought his used Volkswagen camper and set off with the Orlovskys to explore America and read to students in the hinterlands. He had been out of the country, for the most part, since 1961, and, he says, he was eager to see "what was happening with American kids." In Prague that past May Day, some hundred thousand Czech students had crowned him King of the May and borne him through the streets of the city in a rose-covered chariot. (Ginsberg ruled in Prague until someone—the father of one of the students, the Prague police said—swiped a notebook diary that Ginsberg must have dropped at a concert and turned it over to the police; four hours later, Ginsberg was on a plane to London accused of having "abused Czechoslovakian hospitality and grossly violated the norms of decent world behavior.") Then, in London, seven thousand students had appeared for what turned out to be a historic poetry-reading marathon at the Albert Hall. Now Ginsberg was wondering whether American students had also "awakened" during the years of his wanderings. For the next five months, the camper rattled back and forth across the prairie, and—while rock blared on the radio, various hitchhikers snored on the back seats, and Orlovsky, behind the wheel, kept up a murmuring, playful conversation with the car—Ginsberg contemplated the Middle West with the enthusiasm of a missionary approaching Borneo. The students, in turn, contemplated Ginsberg. Most of them knew of him more as a legendary beatnik from the fifties than as the philosopher-king of a seminal hippiedom, and at first they came to his readings primarily to get a look at him—and in the slim hope that Ginsberg, if provoked, would take off his clothes. (Ginsberg had taken off his clothes in 1957 at a poetry reading in Los Angeles: "Gregory Corso was trying to read his poem 'Power,'" he says, "and somebody got up and said, 'What are you guys trying to prove?' so I interrupted and said 'Nakedness.' There was a drunk in the back of the room—it was a private house—and he said, 'What do you mean, nakedness?' So I took off my clothes. Everybody got very upset, but the one thing, taking off my clothes just that one time, probably communicated a great deal because I keep hearing about it years later. I'm the poet who took off his clothes at a poetry reading. No—who *always* takes off his clothes at poetry readings.")

Ginsberg had to work at converting the children of Kansas and Nebraska. He taught them how to chant ("Try '*Om a ra batsa na de de de de*,' it's a mantra to preserve memory, a scholarly mantra"); talked about ecstasy with what was apparently a disarming reasonableness; patiently answered their questions about his love life; corrected their poetry ("Remember what William Carlos Williams said: No ideas but in things"); taught them Eastern philosophy; sent them off to the library to read Blake, Pound, Catullus, and Kerouac; counseled them on how not to get drafted ("Make it inconvenient for them to take you, tell them you love them, tell them you slept with *me*"); organized their protests; and told them to be nice to their parents ("Don't run to your mother and shout, 'I saw God and you didn't.' After all, she gave birth to you, so she must have been *somewhere*").

Just before Ginsberg left the Midwest, a girl at one of his readings happened to ask if he had been having a good time. "It's been groovy," Ginsberg replied. "I've gotten some feeling for all of you and where you're at"—then he thought for a minute —"but I haven't gotten laid yet, so I've missed the opportunity to know *one* of you really well, to explore *that* kind of a relationship."

The students of Nebraska appeared to find this an entirely reasonable grievance. They said that they were beginning to wonder why none of their other teachers respected them enough to talk to them that way.

By the time Ginsberg came home to New York in the spring of 1966, the Allen Ginsberg poster—Ginsberg as Uncle Sam— was selling out in hard-core corn-belt department stores, and invitations to read were pouring into his box in the Peter Stuyvesant post office. He reported to his friends that there were omens of change. "Like in Kansas," he told his father a week or so after the trip. "The English department refused to sponsor me but the philosophy department agreed. The *philosophy* department. Then the chancellor warned that he would stop me if I said dirty words, and so the vice squad came armed with tape recorders, but *they* left weeping. And the students—they were confused, but they were friendly, hopeful, *adorable*. They were beginning to groove."

At the end of 1966, Ginsberg hired a manager. His friends were astounded, but Ginsberg says that he found the idea of a poet with a manager "charming." The manager, whose name was Charles Rothschild, handled Ginsberg's friend Bob Dylan and a good many other performers, and Ginsberg clearly preferred him to the sedate lecture-series bureaus that traditionally arranged readings for poets. While Ginsberg took care of invitations from college literary magazines and fledgling poetry centers, Rothschild booked him for maximum exposure—at places like the Westbury Music Fair in Long Island, where he split the bill with the Butterfield Blues Band, and at the Santa Monica Auditorium, where he went on with the Fugs. During the first five months of 1967, Ginsberg read, chanted, lectured, and debated close to forty times. Reading his poetry, he went from Berkeley to San Francisco State and the University of California at Davis and at Santa Cruz, then on to Muhlenberg, the University of Illinois, the University of Wisconsin at Milwaukee, the University of Chicago, Northwestern, Michigan State, Wayne State, Washington University, Cornell, the University of New Brunswick, in Canada, Boston University, Simmons, Vanderbilt, East Tennessee State, Oberlin, the University of Southern California, the University of New Mexico, east again to the State University of New York at Stony Brook, Drew University, Paterson State, and Jersey City State, and, finally, to Kenyon, the University of Iowa, the University of Wisconsin, Oregon State, the University of Oregon, Portland State, and Western Washington State. There were also the dates in Westbury and Santa Monica, a psychedelic festival in Toronto, Valentine's Day in the East Village, a scattering of Be-Ins, drug debates at New York University and the Manhattan Junior League, an evening of chant instruction for the drop-outs at Timothy Leary's New York League for Spiritual Discovery, a television session in Chicago, a benefit chant for a psychedelic night club called the Balloon Farm, on St. Mark's Place, and a week with the Indians at the Santo Domingo Pueblo reservation in New Mexico.

This time, Ginsberg came home to report that the country was ripe for a concerted attack of tenderness. He said that he had encountered the usual policemen hovering around the back of campus auditoriums, sniffing the air for the unmistakable smell of pot and waiting for an obscenity to drop, but that for once no one had tried to arrest him and one policeman had actually inquired how long it would take to grow a Ginsberg beard. At Marquette, after a century of conservative Catholic quiet, a ban on a Ginsberg reading by the Jesuit fathers who run the university had produced in very short order a national academic scandal, complete with the dropping of the renewal options on several faculty contracts, a protest investigation into speakers' rights, a burgeoning free-speech movement on the campus, daily retaliatory editorials in the administration-supported college newspaper ("But to say that the student, for example, is free to investigate Communism is not to say at the same time that he is free to establish a party cell on campus"), and a mass rally of students, who marched five miles in the rain to Wisconsin at Milwaukee, where the reading finally was held. A few days later, the battle lines were drawn at Michigan State when the campus police stopped the sale of Ginsberg's books at a benefit reading that he gave for *Zeitgeist*, the campus literary magazine. His thank-you note from Charles Page, the provost of Stevenson College at the University of California at Santa Cruz ("Personally, I was rather surprised by the poem with which you led off; it came as something of a shock to many of us who carry a burden of conventionality, including at least some of the students in the audience"), had been mild enough, considering some of the mail that he *used* to receive from college administrators. The English teacher from New Jersey State who had introduced him and then grabbed the microphone back to shout, "This evening does not receive the endorsement of the English department," was more to be pitied than despised, Ginsberg said. And as for the lady who had called him up in the course of a phone-in-and-talk-to-tonight's-guest radio program on the West Coast and screamed, "Ginsberg, you're nothing but a *douche bag*," he had been so charmed by *her* inventiveness that he went around for weeks quoting the metaphor. Ginsberg, who once had wept to discover himself on the cover of the London *Daily Mail* as "one of the most vicious characters in America" (he shared the title with Corso, William Burroughs, and Jack Kerouac), could only conclude that either he was mellowing or people, spiritually, were "in a better bag." At any rate, two weeks later he was off on another reading tour.

These reading marathons—and the fact that four more Ginsberg books were due to come out if the poet found time to edit them—put Ginsberg in what for him was the uncomfortable position of making money. Ever since the fifties, when he swore off work to become a full-time poet, Ginsberg had been living entirely to his taste on a few thousand dollars a year—at first because he never had any more than that, and later because he liked life "simple," suspected that profit was an unfriendly concept, and had strong misgivings about paying taxes to a government at war. (When an accountant, whom he acquired along with his manager, checked Ginsberg's records last year for possible back taxes, all he could come up with was that Ginsberg's lifetime Social Security payments were approximately a hundred and twenty-five dollars in arrears.) "Diogenes the cynic, rejecting the ordinary goods of life, family, vocation, and material comforts" was the way one of Ginsberg's critics described him. His friends preferred to think of him as a sort of latter-day Hebrew prophet, roaming raggedy, exhortative, and penitential among the idol-worshipers. Ginsberg himself apparently never wasted much time wondering why he enjoyed being poor. For years he refused to take money for his readings, insisting that they either be benefits or admission-free. (Orlovsky still refuses to read for money, and, in fact, to have his poems published; he says that poems should be "gifts.") When Ginsberg felt like traveling, there were always fellow-poets and shamans around to feed him and take him in. His own home, which is a fourth-floor walk-up, cost sixty dollars and forty-nine cents a month, and the royalties on his books—they were the standard paperback royalties—always came to enough to pay the rent. Any money that was left over he gave away. His philanthropic dealings, which had a certain carefree, cavalier quality about them, usually consisted of his rummaging through his pockets for loose change while a friend waited at the door. Now, as a tycoon of sorts—"My God, like I stand to make thirty thousand dollars next year," he told a friend in Berkeley, who was horrified—and, given his enthusiasms, a man of particular interest to the government, he was advised to do his sharing with a little more regard for the legal proprieties. And so, in 1966, Ginsberg became a charitable, tax-exempt foundation. Ginsberg's older brother, Eugene, who is a lawyer on Long Island, drew up the foundation charter. Orlovsky was named president. Edward Sanders, the poet and lead Fug, became vice-president. Ginsberg, under the circumstances, wanted to be treasurer, and his brother, as an attorney, took the job of secretary. After innumerable alternative names, including the Ginsberg Foundation, were discarded as either terrible or inappropriate, Ginsberg was formally incorporated that March as the Committee on Poetry—a name that had proved useful over the years in adding cachet to the various public protests he liked to issue from his apartment. "This group," his charter began, "is formed to gather money from those that have it in amounts excess to their needs and disburse it among poets and philosophers who lack personal finance or wherewithal to accomplish small material projects in the society at large. The committee's money will be used to sustain artists and their projects in times of stress; promote freedom of expression where such expression is threatened by social prejudice or outside force; publish works of art which have no immediate commercial vehicles for publicity; aid sick, wounded or nervous creative souls who might otherwise be financially isolated; participate in projects for altering the consciousness of the Nation toward a more humane spirit of Adhesiveness prophesied by Whitman; give joy to writers and artists who wish to escape unpleasant circumstances and travel or meditate; help unlucky poets and painters avoid confinement in jails and madhouses or ease their return to freedom; and otherwise aid in spiritual emergencies."

Ginsberg, who now was the only Guggenheim poet with a foundation of his own, started giving money away immediately. He opened a special Committee account at his local bank on Avenue B—loose Committee cash around the house was deposited in a special pocket of an old tweed sports coat—and his friends began to notice that Ginsberg, on his tours, was developing a lively new interest in being paid. At the end of the year, Ginsberg instructed Rothschild to get him "the full, going rate for famous people." (That next spring, at a dinner in his honor at Boston University, Ginsberg learned that Senator Strom Thurmond, of South Carolina, had preceded him in the school's Distinguished Lecture Series. Ginsberg peered at the students who had hired him. "Thurmond's on the wrong side—what did *he* get?" he said.)

In 1967, Ginsberg, who was still living on his royalties, was able to put some twenty thousand dollars into the Committee checking account. He paid his agent, his accountant, and the repair bill on his tape recorder, and then he quickly got rid of the rest of the money as one spiritual emergency after another happened to arise. Four thousand dollars went to Ginsberg's filmmaker friend Jack Smith—Smith was responsible for the transvestite epics *Flaming Creatures* and *Norman Love*, and his "pursuit of similar exemplary manifestations," according to Ginsberg, had been interrupted by a marijuana conviction now on appeal in the federal courts. Twenty-five hundred dollars made the first payment on twenty-four acres of a large tract of Sierra lowland—the rest of it is owned by Ginsberg's friends Gary Snyder and Dick Baker, a Zen Buddhist retreat director who organizes poetry conferences at Berkeley, and a Hindu convert from Scarsdale who goes by the name Kryananda—for the use of any nervous, creative soul who might want to camp there, build a hut and work, or simply get away. The Committee paid four hundred dollars for the tanka for Bowen's "indigenous psychedelic ashram" in the Haight-Ashbury, on the condition that it pass to the Mahalila, a sacred orgy community across the Golden Gate Bridge in Marin County, if the ashram never managed to materialize. Fifteen hundred dollars went to Maretta, for her spiritual pilgrimage to Outer Mongolia, and another fifteen hundred apiece to Gregory Corso and Herbert Huncke, as writers' grants-in-aid. Irving Rosenthal, who edits many of the avant-garde poets and novelists, got twenty-five hundred dollars to continue *his* work. Harry Smith, another film maker, got fifteen hundred, and Ken Kesey got four hundred dollars to start a movie of his own. Smaller grants were awarded— Ginsberg loves saying "awarded"—to LeRoi Jones, who was appealing a two-and-a-half to three-year prison sentence for carrying two loaded pistols during the 1967 Newark riots; to Bob Brannerman, an artist in California; to an underground London paper called the *International Times*; to the poets Ray Bremser, Diana Di Prima, and Charles Plymell; to a film-maker friend named Barbara Rubin, who made Maretta's culottes; and to Lee Myersove, in San Francisco, who puts out a Jewish literary quarterly called the *Burning Bush*. The Committee also paid the bill at the Hotel Chelsea when Basil Bunting came to town to read his poetry at the Guggenheim and when a young Benali poet who was in residence at the Writers Workshop at the University of Iowa wanted to spend a week in New York. It bought a new harmonium for Swami Bhaktivedanta's New York ashram; a twenty-dollar set of building blocks, from F. A. O. Schwartz, for a group of visiting Indian Ballad Singers to play with, and four records of Vedic chanting for Ezra Pound. And, after a visiting literary Digger spent the night at Ginsberg's apartment, it voted to cover $3.26 of that month's telephone bill.

Appropriately, the question of Ginsberg's money was considered by the Diggers at a meeting in the Haight-Ashbury that spring. The meeting had been called by means of a crytic mimeographed bulletin declaring a state of community emergency. After six months of psychedelic social work, the Diggers had come to the conclusion that everybody in the neighborhood but them was either making money for himself or holding on to whatever he already had, and now they wanted a showdown, "to straighten out the bad money bag."

Emmet Grogan, a hot, glowering Digger out of an O'Casey

play, had the floor when Ginsberg walked into the recreation room in Glide Church, where the meeting was held.

"The Diggers have a demand, and that's that the rest of you— all the bands, stores, and people in *this* whole fucking hippie scene—go nonprofit," Grogan was screaming. "That means if you're a store you take that money you make and share it with the people who make your beads and sandals. We want you to start living this love shit you're always talking about."

Ginsberg raised his hand. He told the hippies how they could turn into foundations like him, and he added, to Grogan, "What does a guy like me do who's making some bread and decides he wants to buy a little piece of land? I just bought some groovy Committee on Poetry land, and like now I think I'd like a little of something for myself." Ginsberg waited for a reaction. "*Just* for myself," he said.

"Hey, listen, man, money's guilt," Grogan yelled. "Let's cut the money. Say I make beads and you make sandals—we'll *trade* them."

"What do you want me to do, carry my poems around and trade them?" Ginsberg said.

"Yeah, Emmet," one of the psychedelic shopkeepers at the meeting broke in. He was wearing a tie and jacket, and by community standards he looked prosperous.

Grogan snarled at him.

"Seriously, Emmet," the shopkeeper said, "who's going to decide how much each of Allen's poems is worth? Allen's demands might be more than yours."

"Allen wants to make fifteen thousand a year?" Grogan snapped. "Let him make it. *I* won't talk to him."

"It's not money, it's *seeds* that are important," a boy called from under one of the church's Ping-Pong tables. Several hippies cheered and rang their bells, and the boy crawled out. He was draped in strings of radishes, and there was a corncob hanging from the belt of his blue jeans. "I'm sure if we knew the divine secret of putting a seed in the ground and making it grow, we'd be cured of money," he said.

"I'm sure that's what Allen meant when he said he wanted to buy some land," one of the hippie maidens interrupted. "He wants to learn the divine secret of making things grow."

Ginsberg laughed. "No, I just want a piece of property," he said.

"Allen's just a rich Jewish merchant," Grogan yelled.

Michael Bowen, who had been leaning against a wall sketching mandalas in an account ledger, ran to the front of the room and confronted him. "Poets don't care about money," Bowen said. "Poets can stand on the corner and talk to telephone poles all day and stay happy. They get something out of telephone poles, man."

"No," Ginsberg said again. "I want some money. Like, I'd rather talk to a tree than a telephone pole."

"Listen," Grogan shouted. "Suppose I go to the woods. You mean I'm going to see Allen Ginsberg up some tree, chanting and waving some gong around? Wow! I think I'm lost, and I see Ginsberg talking to a tree. Who needs that?"

"Hear, hear," Ginsberg said. "I've got my bag. I just want to be left alone."

Chapter 3

"Hey, I want to give this lecture," Ginsberg warned the red, bawling baby girl in a leather basket on her mother's hip. It was the afternoon of Ginsberg's fourth day at Berkeley, and he was sitting cross-legged on top of a big oak teacher's desk in Room 123 of Wheeler Hall, conducting a seminar. On the blackboard behind him there were chains of thick, mysterious equations left over from an advanced mathematics class that morning. In front of him, in writing-slab schoolchairs, all over the floor, and on every available inch of radiator cover and windowsill, there were Berkeley undergraduates—about a hundred of them—taking notes. The staid, regulation-tan classroom was lit with paisley shirts, Indian ponchos, and bright, short skirts. The boys had floppy manes of hair, and one girl, in a red burlap tunic, was meditating on a spray of flowers. The baby continued to cry.

"Maybe I sound scary or something," Ginsberg suggested. "I woke up grumpy this morning. My old friend Orlovsky had cut off two feet of his hair and taken off for New York. My first response was anger. Like I thought he was on some kick and that *that* was the reason for his behavior. Then, when it was too late, I realized that I had an opportunity to find out what was really the matter, but instead I had run around slamming windows and shouting, 'What the fuck is going on?' My awareness was turned off. I was acting on inadequate data, on a big ego thing." Ginsberg thought for a moment. "That's what governments do. Like, that's the whole trouble with China."

"What does this say in terms of your search for the divinity within, sir?" a small voice from somewhere on the floor asked Ginsberg.

Ginsberg followed the sound until he came to a boy who was stretched out on a striped poncho. "I say stop being so sentimental," Ginsberg said.

The boy sat up. "Of course divinity has nondivinity as its correlate," he began again.

"I guess you could say that," Ginsberg said, smiling.

"What I *mean* is you look for divinity within and find divinity without. How's that?" the boy said. He looked hopeful.

"You know how Ramakrishna once described what divinity— no, it was bliss—felt like?" Ginsberg said. "Like the tongues of angels licking honey off his asshole."

A number of the undergraduates murmured, "Beautiful."

"That, of course, would be divinity, or bliss, experienced in the first chakra, which is a specific devotional body center." Ginsberg added quickly. "The Mahayana Buddhists have seven of them. The second one is about, let's see, roughly two inches below the belly button"—Ginsberg located his navel and measured down—"and the third is around your solar plexus. That's where power comes from. The fourth is the heart chakra, used for purposes of adoration. Then there's the mouth, which is intellect, thought, reason. And the *sixth* chakra, which is like a really wild groovy one, is the third-eye chakra." Ginsberg pointed to his forehead. "It's the seat of dreams and archetypes. Also the imagination, fantasy, inner-space travel. And the last one is the top-of-the-head chakra, which is like *real* bliss, because it's where the soul escapes at death." Ginsberg stopped and scratched his own head. "Now what was the question?"

"I forgot," the boy on the poncho said.

"What's with this Swami Bhaktivedanta you've been hanging around with, Allen?" a boy with bells in the pockets of his blue jeans called out from the back of the room, where he was relaxing with his head on the stomach of a young lady from the philosophy department.

"I just dig his mantra, that's all," Ginsberg said. "*Hare Krishna* happens to be a particular mantra I groove with. Like you can use it as a vehicle for any passion that you feel. Bhakti yoga is what you call it, and Krishna's like whatever you know. You can call it Krishna or shit, but if you say it a million times, it'll make the universe tremble. There's one mantra for destroying a god. You have to say *that* one ten million times."

"Explain Krishna *exactly*," a girl who was lying on her back with her eyes closed asked him. She was wearing paint-splattered blue jeans and an artist's smock with a big "Orgy Organizer" button pinned to it, and she had long red hair, which spread out behind her on the floor. Several of the boys in the class were staring at her.

"Krishna's like a friend-lover-helper-LSD-supervisionary prince," Ginsberg said. "There are others you can sing to. Like Vishnu, the preserver, who comes back whenever a bomb or a flood is about to take over and who's usually shown as a fish or a turtle or a lion, and in one really groovy interesting picture as a sexy human body with a big ugly boar's head. And there's Rama, who is like a godly nineteenth-century Krishna incarnation and is a kind of Prince Hal sort of guy, only more princely, more responsible. I just happen to like Krishna best —I guess because he's a lover. He has a blue body, and he was a cowboy. Like when he was a kid he had a cow to take care of. Later, he had Rada, his girl friend. So you can think of him as either a pure divine lover or a sex lover." Ginsberg chuckled. "I wouldn't exactly say that Bhaktivedanta thinks of Krishna as a big blue sexy cowboy. Sex is not his yoga."

The boy on the poncho waved his hand. "You throw out all this yoga, but before, when I asked, you were saying that you were down on looking within."

"It was in that particular context," Ginsberg said. "I found it not very meaningful, so I bridled." Ginsberg stopped to wave good-bye to the bawling baby, who had been fastened into her basket and was in the process of being hurried out of the room. He told her that her chance "to be a big Berkeley professor like me and make a lot of noise" would come in time. Three boys climbed through an open window, momentarily dislodging some windowsill sitters, and crawled toward the abandoned floor space. Ginsberg asked them if there were any more students listening from the lawn, and when they nodded, he ordered all the other windows opened.

"I'm sick of talking about chanting," Ginsberg said, after everyone had scrambled in. "I talked about chanting *yesterday*."

"Talk about Dylan Thomas," a boy in chinos and a sports coat said. "Did you ever meet him?"

"Yeah, once, by accident," Ginsberg said, and he added, "I like 'Fern Hill'—it's something like 'Intimations of Immortality' —but on the whole I don't really dig Thomas. He's too romantic. With his kind of gift, the way to groove was to begin with bricks and build a starry tower, but Thomas *began* in a starry tower. I guess I think that he and Hart Crane were killed by their own intentions. They tried to re-create the unconscious through rational conscious means, so maybe they had to drink to get at it. They didn't follow what Stein said—that like the mind is goofy enough itself if you only listen to it. They were too influenced by people like Keats and Yeats and Bridges"—the class groaned—"and Hopkins, whereas poets like me are based on Stein and Pound and Whitman and Williams."

"I still think Crane's a groove," the boy in chinos said.

"And I say if Crane had had a chance to goof around in the Haight-Ashbury he never would have died," Ginsberg said.

"Naw, Crane couldn't have *ever* lived," the boy said.

"But he *could* have lived," Ginsberg cut in. "If somebody had only grabbed his cock—if he'd had enough boy friends or girl friends or whatever it was he liked. And if somebody had turned him on, to get him off lush. Instead, he had this *heavy* literary environment on his back."

"What about Bob Dylan? How does he create?" the girl with the flowers asked, patting a silvery, stickummed third eye securely into place in the middle of her forehead.

"Just by goofing around at the typewriter with a piece of paper," Ginsberg replied, sounding enthusiastic.

"He's a great poet," the girl said.

"Everybody thinks so except for a few prissy, jealous, second-rate poets," Ginsberg agreed. "I don't know one *real* poet who doesn't think he's a genius. He's like Brecht, or Rimbaud. At his worst, every fourth line of Dylan's is a line of genius, and that's better than most. Dylan returned poetry to where it was in Elizabethan times. To song. To Campion and Waller." Ginsberg looked around. "Does anybody know Pound's 'ABC of Reading'?" he said.

The students shook their heads.

"What's the matter, don't they teach Pound at this place?" Ginsberg asked them.

The students shook their heads again.

Ginsberg shrugged. "Well," he began, "Pound points out that measurement of line in poetry started with the Greek choruses, singing and dancing across the stage. It had something *real* attached to it." Ginsberg jumped down and began dancing around his desk, singing the beginning of "Oedipus Rex" and stamping his left foot on every downbeat. "You see," he said after a few turns. "Like *that*."

The class applauded.

"Take the music away and how do you measure?" Ginsberg went on. "How do you even *pronounce*? The line begins to be da *da* da *da* da *da*, and soon the emotions begin to be da *da* da *da* da *da*." Ginsberg stopped to catch his breath. "Maybe there's some sixteen-year-old kid in a place like Wichita right now who's not just writing but singing and dancing his poetry," he said. "That's what *I'd* like to see—the first poetry reading where a naked sixteen-year-old kid from Wichita comes on singing and dancing poetry."

Ginsberg climbed back onto the desk and then asked the class if anybody had a cigarette. The girl on her back reached into a huge thonged shoulder bag on the floor beside her and tossed a pack of Gauloises up to Ginsberg. He said *"Om,"* took two, and tossed back the pack. The girl opened her eyes and smiled.

"Hasn't *anybody* here read Pound?" Ginsberg said. "You're *sure*? That's really amazing. There ought to be enough scholars around here who'd be willing to look up all the references."

"But that's bad, man—like you have to go to the library to look up references," a young man in a First World War British infantry officer's jacket replied.

"But the things that Pound turns you on to are *groovy*," Ginsberg said. "Like Pound on gold. You know that Pound went to the bughouse after he discovered that if you had gold you could use it for credit at a rate of sixteen to one. Just the gold people could do that. Not the silver people or the poetry people or the tree people." Ginsberg looked around hopefully. "Pound can put you on to a lot of fascinating gossip like that," he said. "He was like a big influence on me. Williams too. Before I met Williams, I was all hung up on cats like Wyatt, Surrey, and Donne. I'd read them and then copy down what I thought poetry like theirs would be. Then I sent some of those poems to Williams, and he thought that they were terrible. Like, they showed some promise, but they were phony, unnatural. He told me, 'Listen to the rhythm of your own voice. Proceed intuitively by ear.' *His* praxis was listening for all the funny things going on around him—like the Italian workmen in Paterson saying 'I'll kick yuh eye' to each other. In a way, he was like Cézanne, who was like a big tea-head, running around observing the optical phenomena and then trying to re-create them. Anyway, the next thing I sent Williams was some observations, jotted down in a bus, and when he saw *them* he said, 'Yeah, that's where it's at!' or the equivalent. He started me carrying around a notebook, writing down whatever I heard and saw."

"Like in that poem you read the other night, where you threw in all those place names and headlines and comics," a boy who was hanging from a sash cord on one of the windows called to Ginsberg.

"Well, *there* it was a little confusing," Ginsberg said. "Like I didn't know what I was doing, so I just had to depend on whatever data was coming in."

"Were you high?" the boy asked him.

"Oh, maybe occasionally, on pot," Ginsberg said.

"Poems like that—do you think they'll survive?" the boy asked, sliding onto the window sill.

Ginsberg unfolded himself into a sort of semi-squat and yanked at the knot of his flowered tie. "That's a problem," he said finally. "There are some pretty things in them. I don't know. Maybe they'll be valuable as like big important historical documents. Maybe somebody'll put them in a time capsule and some American-history student in the year 3000 will dig them up and say, 'Look, guys, there was this weird place, Nebraska, where people needed radios and newspapers to tune in on what was happening. And there was this cat named Rex Morgan who turned up every Sunday in four colors to complain about some kind of pill everybody was taking called LSD.' " Ginsberg shrugged. "I'm just a transitional character. Like I'm not back to music like Dylan or that Wichita poet who'll be around for your generation."

"Donovan's making the poetry-music scene now, better than Dylan even," the boy with the bells in his pockets called out. He rolled off his friend's stomach and stood up, so that Ginsberg could get a look at him.

"I dig Donovan," Ginsberg said.

"What about Stockhausen and Cage?" the girl on her back said. "Do you relate to *them*? I really relate to them."

"I could," Ginsberg replied. "I guess it's a little hard at first. It's like people getting used to Indian music. I like Stockhausen, though. I worked in a Happening with him once, and he was very human. Like he put this gigantic electronic fart into the middle of his symphony."

"I find it easier to lose myself in Bach than in Stockhausen," the girl who was meditating on the flowers announced, with a small shiver of pleasure.

"I get hung up on Bach too," Ginsberg told her. "Sometimes I think that if people listened to one little piece by Bach as often in a month as they listen to 'Sad-Eyed Lady of the Lowlands,' they'd maybe find they were connecting with Bach too."

"Yeah, but with classical music you just sit there," the boy from the First World War broke in. "With rock-and-roll you get to move around."

"That's what I like about rock-and-roll," Ginsberg said. "It's like the Afro-Cuban music. It has a physical impact on the body. Like, it involves the pelvis and the belly. There's a Yoruba dance to Chango—he's a Siva-like god, also very groovy—that's like a kind of two-step rustle, and it's got some of the same feeling as a lot of what's been coming out of Liverpool." Ginsberg rocked back and forth on the oak desk, his hands planted on his knees, humming a cheery "Kyrie."

The meditative young lady looked up very slowly from her flowers. "I'm afraid that with rock-and-roll my energy diffuses and will not return to its original source," she said, with a wistful smile. "It's like that for me with all ethnic music. My vital energy is affected."

"Maybe that's because ethnic music—like rock-and-roll is really just *urban* ethnic music—appeals to the lower chakra. *Physically* lower, that is," Ginsberg suggested. "Maybe a refined rock-and-roll could move up the body and open the heart chakra. Sometimes Dylan does that. Try listening to *him*."

"Artaud thought that music could actually have a psychochemical effect on you," a boy in a blue knit beanie with a big pompon on it told the girl.

Ginsberg looked surprised. He asked the boy in the beanie how he happened to know about Artaud.

The boy in the beanie said that he had read all about Artaud in an old Ginsberg interview in the *Paris Review*. "Do you groove with Kenneth Burke, Allen?" he asked. "He knows a lot about music too."

Ginsberg shook his head.

The boy in the beanie said, "Gee, as far as I'm concerned, Burke's the greatest mind since Aristotle."

"I never dug Aristotle," Ginsberg remarked.

The boy in the beanie said that he was writing an English paper on hippie talk, based on Burke's theory of language as symbolic action.

"You too?" a girl in the row behind him said, leaning forward to look at him. "I'm doing hippie talk for my anthropology thesis."

"You'll have to include other kinds of hippie communication, then," Ginsberg told her. "Like their family-sex communication arising through orgy."

"They call that *family*?" the girl asked.

"Why not?" Ginsberg said, laughing.

"Then that's *their* bag," the girl said.

" 'Bag' is so pejorative," Ginsberg said. "Like 'beatnik.' "

The boy in the beanie raised his hand. "But didn't the word 'beatnik' consolidate you, like bring you all together?" he asked, and then, brightening, added, "Didn't it work as a kind of symbolic action?"

"Hell, no," Ginsberg said. "It created a whole lot of semantic problems and got everybody upset."

"That's always the problem with language," the young lady with the flowers concurred.

"No, it's the problem of the society," a boy on one of the radiator covers cut in.

"It's actually more the problem of the way society constructs its hierarchies of values," the boy in the beanie said.

Ginsberg threw up his hands. "That's the kind of thing I never dug about Burke," he said. "Like what does that *mean*?"

The boy in the beanie shook his head.

"Well, I guess by now negative understanding of anybody's problems is irrelevant anyway," Ginsberg said. "The question is what do we *do*. The question's political."

"But how can you have a political Buddha?" the boy on the radiator said.

"You know the Bodhisattva vow?" Ginsberg asked him. "A Bodhisattva is someone capable of entering Nirvana but—"

"Who vows to save all sentient beings," the boy said. " 'Sentient beings are numberless, I vow to save them all. The gates of the dharma are endless, I vow to enter them all. Passions are numberless, I vow to extinguish them all.' " He looked at Ginsberg, who was smiling. "Did I get it right?"

Ginsberg nodded.

"So where are *you* in all this, Allen?" the boy said.

"Me? I'm just working away," Ginsberg told him, swinging out his legs and contemplating his shoes, which needed polishing again. "Actually, I'm overworked. I need to get away. I'd like a place in the country where I can clear my head, so I can come back to the city and maybe accomplish something." He shrugged. "I get this Dostoevskian urge to get back to New York and confront, say, Lionel Trilling. Also, there are sentient beings in the city. Are you going to abandon them for your little nirvana? *That* doesn't lead to bliss. Like there was this meeting in the Haight-Ashbury the other night, and the kids were all scream-

ing about the cops and the city and how the city was a bad bag
and how they had to desert it for the country to save their souls.
But the thing was they wouldn't know how to build themselves
a shelter in the country to get away *to*. They have no compe-
tence. That's what gets them all fucked up and sends them
screaming naked through plate-glass windows so that they have
to spend time and money bailing each other out of jails and
bughouses. And then they blame it all on *cities!*" Ginsberg took
a deep breath. "Does that make any sense?"

"So are you optimistic or pessimistic?" the boy on the radiator
asked him.

Ginsberg burst out laughing. "That's obvious," he said. "What
are you doing with a beard, and what am I doing with a tie?"

"Come on, Allen, what do you *propose*?" the boy said.

"Well, I propose that things in common are much more important than distinctions," Ginsberg began, jumping off the
desk and picking up his jacket, which was on the floor. "I propose that the war is bad. I propose that the educational structure
is wrong, the curriculum is wrong, the people in charge wrong.
I propose civil liberties and the individual right to speech and
sex as against a police state. I propose the sexual commune as
an intelligent, spiritual way of life as against a kind of dinosaur
Socialism run by a bunch of sexually and spiritually perverted
Marxists. I propose that we avoid any organization which is
top-heavy and authoritarian. I propose that mystical types beware
of god-gurus and the politicos beware of dictators. I propose that
Tim Leary and Stokely Carmichael get together and cook up
something for Mississippi and Alabama." Ginsberg grinned.
Then, waving his jacket at the ceiling, he hollered, "I propose
that the Apocalypse will turn out to be some big, cheerful pruning
exercise. That for a while we'll be all one self, sharing the self-i-
ness of things. And that everybody who survives will wake up
sexy and refreshed and saying, 'Look, guys, it's *me* again!'"

Chapter 4

In 1945, when Ginsberg was a sophomore at Columbia College, the windows of his room in Hamilton Hall got dirty, and this began to worry him. For days, he says, he woke with a fresh hope that the pious Irish scrub who was assigned to Hamilton would rescue his windows with her sudsy bucket, but he came home from classes every afternoon to find them one shade darker than the afternoon before. It apparently never occurred to Ginsberg—who says that he felt neglected above all students—to wash his own windows, and he brooded about his unhappy karma until he hit upon a plan to force the maid's hand. He etched a number of rather graphic pictures into the grime on the window-panes, and captioned them explicitly, with a pithy imputation as to the endowments of Nicholas Murray Butler, who was president of Columbia then, and—Ginsberg says for irony's sake—the legend "Fuck the Jews." Then he waited. The maid held out, but a few days later Ginsberg was suspended by the dean. "My career at Columbia was like never an ordinary one," Ginsberg has since said. At the time of the suspension, he was studying history to prepare for law school and getting A's on his report cards, and he was also running the Philolexian Society, editing *The Jester*, and enjoying a modest campus reputation as a mad but friendly genius, a man who had been conquered by West Point in the debate "Should Armies and Navies Be Permanently Abandoned?" and one of the most irrepressibly troublesome characters in the school. His troubles with Dean Nicholas McKnight, who ruled over the undergraduate school and was referred to by Ginsberg and his friends as Woodrow Wilson, began earlier that year, with a "disguised" novel about Columbia that was Ginsberg's contribution to a creative-writing course. McKnight found the novel "inappropriate," and, according to the emergency reports he dispatched regularly to Ginsberg's father in New Jersey, he found Ginsberg inappropriate too. Ginsberg was not noted on campus for his tidiness. (The dean was clean-shaven and funereally groomed.) Ginsberg was said to frequent Greenwich Village. He had been involved as a material witness in a campus homicide. His mentors and spiritual advisors were William Burroughs, who lived near Columbia then, and one Herbert Huncke, a combination junkie, mystic, jailbird, and underworld diarist whom Burroughs had discovered hustling on Times Square and, as a sideline, advising Alfred Kinsey on the sexual skills and predelictions of the Square's professional inhabitants. Furthermore, Ginsberg was known to consort with a young writer named Jack Kerouac, whom he had met through friends from the West End Bar and who was banned from the campus at the time as "an unwholesome influence on the students." (Three years earlier, Kerouac had been at Columbia on a football scholarship, which was withdrawn and replaced by a seven-hundred-dollar refectory bill when Kerouac, having broken his tibia, informed Lou Little of the fact that he had come to prefer Mark Van Doren's Shakespeare class to getting beaten up playing games, and quit the team. He was discovered sleeping in Ginsberg's room on the morning of Ginsberg's suspension; Ginsberg paid a $2.63 "overnight guest" fine.)

"When the washerwoman squealed," as Ginsberg tells the story, "McKnight like summoned me and said—I can still hear the words—'Ginsberg, I hope you realize the enormity of what you have done.' I said, 'Oh, I do, sir, I do,' but he had that look in his eyes that meant, 'Ginsberg, I've got you this time.' I felt like I was trapped with a bunch of maniacs. You can't imagine what colleges were like in those days. The whole syndrome of shutdown and provincialism extended to the academy. Like, at Columbia, Whitman was hardly taught and was considered like a creep. Shelley was a creep too. John Crowe Ransom and Allen Tate were like the supreme literary touchstones. Joyce and Lawrence were the property of funny modernist cats like William York Tindall, who was considered eccentric by the rest of the faculty. My course in the American novel went up to Edith Wharton, for some reason. No Gertrude Stein. It was Wharton and Hemingway. So there was no modern literature, in the sense that it would have been considered scandalous to put Henry Miller in the curriculum—not because he was dirty, but because he wasn't even thought of as a writer. Williams was an unknown factor. Like he lived thirteen miles away and was never even invited to read. Pound was taught, but not for his advances or his inventions or his prosody or his understanding of composition. He was taught as a freak-out. The only poet at the school was Van Doren, and even he was writing in a classical style. In economics, they had like Louis Hacker teaching the triumph of capitalism. In history, it was Jacques Barzun who was just teaching politeness. Anthropology was more or less dead. And the French department was filled by old sour-tempered professors whose idea of contemporary French literature was a few reactionary novels written about 1910. And there was a total lack of any sublime teaching. A lack of teachers with praxis for the delicate religious areas that we were approaching *intellectually* in all those seminars on Plotinus and Plato, but never really entering. The only exceptions were Van Doren and Raymond Weaver, who had taught in Japan and used Zen koans in his English class. The rest of the academy was mediocre and incompetent. Almost anything of importance was not taught, and by the time I was suspended I was actually going to Burroughs for all my reading lists."

Burroughs, who had taken a master's degree in anthropology at Harvard in the middle thirties and ever since then had been "just kind of observing things," Ginsberg says, presided over a live-in literary salon of sorts on 115th Street, off Morningside Drive. A girl named Joan Adams, whom Ginsberg and Kerouac had introduced to Burroughs and who later married him, was the lady of the house, and Huncke, Kerouac, and another friend, Hal Chaser, were already living there when Ginsberg joined the family, a few days after leaving Hamilton Hall. Burroughs immediately took over Ginsberg's education, giving him copies of Mayan codices to study, and drilling him on works of the writers they admired—Kafka, Spengler, Blake, Yeats, Céline, Korzybski, Vico, and Rimbaud. Later, Ginsberg began lying down on the living-room couch to free-associate for an hour every day, and Burroughs psychoanalyzed him. (Kerouac's hour came right after Ginsberg's.) For money, Ginsberg took an occasional odd job. He mopped floors at Bickford's, worked in a succession of factories, and eventually shipped out as a messman on a tanker on a few short runs from Bayonne to New Orleans and Galveston and back. He lived at Burroughs' for a year, but by the time he was readmitted to Columbia, the household had begun to break up. Huncke was in and out of jail. Burroughs, who had developed a morphine habit, had been arrested for possession and had fled to Texas, where he married Mrs. Adams (she had been married before), settled down on a little swamp farm in the bayous west of Houston, and began raising fine-grade marijuana. Kerouac went off with Neal Cassady, on the cross-country drive that

he later wrote about in *On the Road*. Ginsberg stayed the semester in New York and then, with a hundred and forty dollars
from a Columbia poetry prize in his pocket, left town to find
his friends. He stopped first in Texas, at the Burroughses', and
from there he caught a bus to Denver, where he, Kerouac, and
Cassady were going to rendezvous. Ginsberg says that being a
lonely college boy who needed love and bringing out and a lot of
attention, he was distressed to find Kerouac distracted and
Cassady absorbed in a new girl friend. They spent what was
an awkward month together, according to Ginsberg, before they
all hitchhiked out of town. Kerouac headed for New York. The
girl went west, toward California. And Ginsberg dropped off
Cassady in Texas, where the Burroughes had just harvested their
first crop and were ready to transport it to the East Coast to sell.
Cassady, during a prison stretch, had learned to make fence posts,
and he was going to mend the Burroughs fences and then drive
the couple to New York. Ginsberg, for his part, was to attend
to making some money. He agreed to ship out from Galveston
and meet them in New York, rich and ready for fall semester,
in a month. The ship, however, turned out to be an old
tanker bound not for Bayonne but for Dakar. Ginsberg, who had
been cataloguing his various sufferings in a long cycle of poems
called *Doldrums*, consoled himself on shipboard by adding his
"Dakar Doldrums" to the others, at the rate of one heroic stanza
a day. He says that he also consoled himself with dreams of
restorative, Gide-like love in the form of a dashing and sympathetic African, but, once in Dakar, his elaborate arrangements
to that effect failed to bridge the language gap with his local
procurer. One night in a back alley, Ginsberg was ceremoniously
presented with a mongolian idiot, whom he had apparently ordered and who had been found only after an exhaustive search
on the part of everybody in the neighborhood. Ginsberg paid
and fled. At the home of a friendly witch doctor, who had come
highly recommended by a shipmate, Ginsberg confessed that his

soul ached. The doctor generously arranged a magic cure at his ceremonial hut, in a bamboo encampment on the edge of town. Ginsberg caught the next tanker home.

Ginsberg's friends had scattered again when he finally arrived in New York late that summer: Cassady had left for California to marry his girl friend, Kerouac had moved to Long Island with his mother, and Burroughs, who was in trouble again, had decided to settle down in Mexico. Ginsberg went back to school, wrote another "Doldrums," and spent the rest of his time rereading Dostoevski. "I wanted to live in a big tragedy-comedy Dostoevskian universe," he says. "That was my ideal. A universe where the characters would all rush up and *confront* each other. A universe where everybody was involved in seeking God and all the heroes were holy idiots. Everybody *else* at Columbia was like very practical and going to business school." Ginsberg says that he spent the next two years "solitary and complaining." Columbia turned down his applications for a graduate fellowship and teaching job. "I was respected at Columbia as a wild poet who smoked pot and liked men and had gotten kicked out of school under extremely glamorous circumstances, but as far as giving me a job—nobody wanted that kind of responsibility," Ginsberg says. The Columbia Broadcasting System, where he went next with the idea of starting out, like Shakespeare, as a stagehand, told him that the sweepers' union had closed its books. *Life* asked him too many questions, and all the advertising agencies he tried said that Ginsberg was not exactly what they had in mind. "I began to get very uptight," Ginsberg says now, "because the tradition was you were supposed to leave Columbia and get a job for seventy dollars a week on a newspaper or in the State Department —something *important* like that—and here I was washing dishes at Bickford's again and having visions." As it happened, Huncke emerged from jail in the course of Ginsberg's last year at college and was back on Times Square, supporting his habit by stealing overcoats and an occasional suitcase from the Pokerino Palace.

Huncke had introduced the word "beat" to Ginsberg, Kerouac, and Burroughs, using it, in the leisurely, philosophical moments he sometimes enjoyed between arrests, to mean exhausted, defeated, and therefore open and unjudging and, in a sense, blessed, and Ginsberg was particularly attached to him. He says that Huncke, who was known to the police at the time as Creep, was the only "truly sophisticated" person left in New York. Ginsberg took him in, and spent the summer of 1948 talking out his troubles while Huncke listened, advised, and began methodically stripping down the Harlem apartment that Ginsberg was subletting from a theologian friend. Huncke started with a rare-book collection—stealing it discreetly, a few volumes at a time. He moved on to the record collection, then to the clothing, and finally to the plates and silverware. After about a month, Ginsberg noticed that the apartment was getting empty. Huncke departed quickly, and Ginsberg began looking for a more adequately furnished place to live. He had found a job in the meantime—his classwork was over—at the Associated Press. It consisted mainly of tearing sheets off teletype machines and delivering them to the proper desks, but it inspired Ginsberg to abandon *Doldrums* for long Blakean poems about the moral complexities of work. ("If money made the mind more sane/ Or money mellowed in the bowel/ The hunger beyond hunger's pain/ Or money choked the mortal growl/ And made the groaner grin again/ Or did the laughing lamb embolden/ To loll where has the lion lain,/ I'd go make money and be golden.") He liked his new apartment, which was on York Avenue and had a huge *National Geographic* globular projection on the living-room wall, and he settled down there to get the final draft of his thesis on "the absolute inside, inner, beyond-language meanings of mythology" typed.

Ginsberg finished Columbia at the end of 1948, under somewhat unusual circumstances.

"Huncke got out of jail again," Ginsberg recalls. "I had told him, like, 'Never darken my door again,' but that kind of thing wasn't part of Huncke's vocabulary, so he found out where I was living and just kind of arrived. It was snowing outside, and his shoes were so bad that his feet were bleeding. He'd been up wandering for four days—the cops had chased him off Times Square—and he was in a funny, almost suicidal state, in a very high state of awareness of things around him, very neurasthenically sensitive and at the same time in a kind of total, somnolent depression. He didn't know where else to go, and I couldn't put him out again, so he got on the couch and stayed there, sleeping, for about three weeks. Then one day he finally went out, to my relief, and came back with some money. He'd robbed a car. I was overjoyed! He'd come back to life. Like he was back operating again, which meant that he wasn't going to die. It was really a very funny, paradoxical situation, because at the time there was all this talk at Columbia about what is right, what is wrong, what's ethics, what's morality, what's social good, what's social bad, what's utilitarianism, what's justifiable, what's unjustifiable —all of it from people who were fighting and scrambling to get ahead and making atom bombs. So I began to notice that Huncke was like a victim of a monstrosity of laws and attitudes. He was a twenty-year addict and in any decent system he would have been pensioned off and supplied with drugs—and how was I in a position to judge whether he was right or wrong in stealing or if he was right or wrong in being an addict? It was beyond that at this point. So with Huncke around, I found my social views altering increasingly through experience. And I began to get that alienated view of the actual structure of society which everybody then thought was disgraceful, but now they call it 'elite alienation' and things like that. Well, Huncke became more and more active, and more and more prosperous. I didn't quite disapprove. I didn't quite approve. I just sort of asked him about it from time to time. I was busy with my own work, writing poems and psalms. Glad that Huncke was alive. But then he began bringing people over to the house. First, there was this

chick I already knew, who had first turned Kerouac and me on to
Benzedrine inhalers. A tall red-headed chick. She had been
mainly a whore, actually, with very expensive johns who would
pay her a hundred dollars a shot. And she was a very lively chick,
who took a lot of pot. Really a remarkable, beautiful, good-
hearted, tender girl. I had a special regard for her from years
before, because she had really put herself out to straighten me
out, and here she was like a big, expensive whore. It had seemed
like an extraordinary gesture. So I wasn't in any position to kick
her out of the house now. She came with her boy friend, a guy
named Little Jack Melody, who was a sort of subdivision cousin
of the Mafia. He was an interesting guy—like he had this Italian
background and a big happy Italian family out on Long Island—
and he was in love with the girl. They were going to have a child.
So it was like a whole *Beggar's Opera* scene at my house. The
three of them were going out on burglary expeditions together,
and bringing back all the loot. They even robbed a detective's
house in Harlem. I remonstrated in vain. There wasn't really
much I could do, and anyway, every time I'd put Huncke down
he'd say, 'What do you want me to do? What am I *supposed*
to do?' So meanwhile my house was filling up with chests of
silver, silver sets, all sorts of dreck like radios, phonograph machines. It was getting crowded, actually. I didn't know what to
do, and I began thinking, 'I've got to kick them out or I've got
to leave myself.' Well, it was too difficult to kick *them* out, and
I really wanted to get away anyway, so I made plans to go down
to Mexico and visit Burroughs. I saved up a little money, and
packed all my stuff in one big set of cardboard boxes. Manuscripts. Letters from Burroughs. Letters from Kerouac. Letters
from Cassady. Everything. Little Jack had a car, and the
plan was that we were going to drive out to Long Island, where
Little Jack would drop off some of his things at his mother's.
Then we'd take all my uptown stuff to store with my brother,
who was at law school at NYU. So we piled everything in the
car—Little Jack, me, and the girl; Huncke stayed home—and

started out toward Long Island, and then, on Utopia Parkway, Little Jack took the wrong turn down a one-way street at the end of which was a police car. Now it so happened that the car we were in was a stolen car. And, in addition to having my papers in it, it had Little Jack's things, which were like a great pile of stolen suits and clothes from the detective's house. So Little Jack, being like a slightly flipped-out Mafia gangster, immediately panicked. And like put his foot down on the gas and instead of just stopping and getting a ticket, tried to outrun the police car. And in the process almost ran over one of the policemen, who were out on the street by now, trying to wave him down. So the police thought Melody was trying to hit them, and *they* immediately panicked, too, and got in *their* car and began chasing us. The next thing I knew, there I was in a car speeding down Utopia Parkway at ninety miles per hour, chased by the police with drawn guns. With Little Jack getting more and more frantic, driving faster and faster and then suddenly swerving the car around, trying to get into a side street, and smashing into a telephone pole. Turning the car over and over and over. And with me having the very distinct sensation, slightly mystical, that all my mistakes of the past year—my moral indecisions and my slight acquisitive interest in some of the loot that was coming into the house—had led in a chain to this one retribution moment where now I was going to have to pay for it. And facing it. Singing as we rolled over in the car, 'Lord God of Israel, Isaac, and Abraham,' from the *Messiah*, like evoking the Hebraic father-figure authority divinity to come and get me, which was a very weird thing. When everything settled down, finally, the car was upside down. My manuscript and all those letters—love letters, incriminating letters about pot from Texas—were swimming around all over the place. And I couldn't find my glasses. I started searching for them, and then I realized that if I didn't beat it I was going to get caught. And I didn't want to get caught yet. Like I might have been able to get out of it then and there

—it wasn't my car and it wasn't my stealing—but my house was full of stolen objects, and the address was in the car all over everything. So—quick thinking—I said, 'I'd better get home immediately. Clean out the house. Phone Huncke.' We had all escaped from the car, actually—the police had overshot the side street and were on their way back—and so we ran off in different directions. The girl got to a friend's house—I don't know how. Little Jack was captured, on the parkway, and beaten up by the police—black and blue. I just sort of wandered off without my eyeglasses down the side street and into a candy store and said, 'How do you get to New York?' They said, 'Are you in a car or what?' So I said, 'I'm a naturalist. And I'm taking a walk with nature.' I only had seven cents in my pocket, and I bummed I think twelve cents more and was able to phone and get a message through to Huncke. And then, somehow or other, I got back to New York—hitchhiking and then the subway, when I had bummed another ten cents—and I walked into the apartment and there was Huncke, looking miserable, like just sort of slowly sweeping the floor. I said, 'What are you doing, Herbert? The police will be here any minute,' but he just said, 'Oh, it's hopeless now. I've been through this so many times. There's nothing you can do.' 'Huncke, for the love of God!' I said, and then bang-bang-bang on the door, and like six big policemen charge in, and some detectives. 'Does Allen Ginsberg live here?' So the next day the New York *Daily News* had a big front-page picture of me and Huncke and the girl coming out of a police car, and the whole situation was transformed from the hermetic, cosmic, nebulous Dostoevskian thing that it was, with like *real* people involved, into this total stereotype of a giant robbery operation —six-foot, marijuana-smoking redhead, three-time-loser pariah criminal, boy-wonder mastermind. Yeah, I was advertised as the brilliant student genius who was like plotting out big criminal scenes. Another newspaper had it that I was addicted to drugs, and this gang kept me supplied and forced me to mastermind robberies. It was all a bunch of awful misinterpretations. By this time my father had come in from New Jersey, weeping, and of course everybody around Columbia was aghast. Like, 'You've made scandals before, Ginsberg, but *this*! And on top of everything, a Columbia student right on the front page of the *Daily News*!' It was really an archetypal scandal. Van Doren felt bad, but like he couldn't really understand it. 'What were you doing with those people?' he said. 'What were you doing with simple common criminals?' And he gave me like a big lecture. He said, 'A lot of us around here have been thinking maybe you'd better hear the clank of iron, Ginsberg. You don't seem to realize what you're doing. If you want my help, you've got to promise never to break the law again.' Which I suppose was very kind of sensible—like work within the society, within the normal structure of society. He posed the problem really very clearly, but at the same time he didn't have the right answer, because I was like saying that if you really felt that people like Huncke were saintly in some way or other, then you should be prepared to suffer for them and go to jail, or *something*. One professor who was really swinging on this, though, was Meyer Schapiro. He said, 'Oh, yeah, so you've been busted. That reminds me of the time *I* went to jail in Europe.' Like he had a completely humane attitude and understood the vicissitudes of poetic life. Lionel Trilling was *horrified* but friendly, helpful, and he took me up to see Professor Herbert Wechsler, at the Law School, to get some advice. The thing Wechsler said was that what I had to do was put myself into a bughouse. Plead insanity and go to a bughouse and get out of all this. So my father got me a lawyer who was an old friend of the family and who was like a real middle-class cat. And it was again like an archetypal situation where a kid gets busted and a lot of middle-class values are offended and the whole family gets excited and says, 'Why does it have to be *our* son? Why does he *do* these things?' And where the lawyer is paternal and helpful but is like saying, 'Abandon everybody! Abandon these terrible

people!' And where the youthful offender, like me, becomes very
confused and unsure of himself and doesn't know what he's doing
and feels like he must have made some terrific cosmic *error*. And
so I was thinking all this time, 'What am I doing? What am I
going through, having visions and ending up in jail? What *is*
reality? Is it my visions, or Huncke's void, or what's actually
going on? Why can't I be like everybody else?' I saw righteous-
ness and sensitivity being persecuted in every direction. And I
was feeling guilty and ashamed because I didn't even go to court,
or *anything*, like the others did, and because they were going to
have to go to jail whereas the charges against me were dropped
and all I had to do was tell some psychiatrist that I heard voices
and had visions and *I* got to go to the Columbia Psychiatric Institute . . . Everything changed the minute I got to the bughouse.
I was sitting in the reception room with my valises, waiting to
be shown a bed, and like all of a sudden I began feeling very
rueful and mad at Huncke, because he was always getting me
into scrapes and he should have known better and protected me.
He shouldn't have put me in this kind of terrible situation. *He*
didn't mind going to jail, but he didn't have to continue the
operation to the point where it actually involved *me*. I didn't
want to be locked up in a bughouse for months and maybe years!
So I was like sitting there and brooding. About how Huncke was
doing bad things like robbing people's cars, inconveniencing people terribly. And about the cruelty of the law, and the ignorance
involved. And about the excessive cruelty of the mass-media people, who were like vultures and harpies. And about the cruelty
of the family apparatus and the cruelty of the criminal apparatus
and my *own* cruelty, making everybody unhappy. And about the
cruelty of the police who had like confiscated my Bhagavad Gita
back at my house, saying, 'We don't allow anything but religious
books in the can,' and about how I kept explaining about the
Bhagavad Gita all the way down to the station. Like it was my
main preoccupation. So I was brooding, when all of a sudden

this guy Carl Solomon—Carl comes up out of the depths of the hospital from a shock streak and waddles over to me. He's in this giant bathrobe, looking very fat because of I think insulin and metrosol. And he looks at me and says, 'Who are *you*?' So I say, 'I'm Myshkin.' 'I'm Kirilov,'" he says."

PART III

"Come home: the pink meat image
   black yellow image with
   ten fingers and two eyes
is gigantic already…"
      —from a poem, "The Change:
      Kyoto–Tokyo Express,
      July 18, 1963," by Allen Ginsberg

Chapter 1

When Ginsberg was a seven-year-old in grammar school, having trouble with multiplication tables and brooding over the fact that a little girl he had kissed behind the bushes on his front lawn had moved to another part of Paterson, a teacher by the name of Miss Morgan restored his confidence. Miss Morgan, according to Ginsberg, was "a spinster lady of the old school." She worshiped books, and one day she decided to give a gold star to every one of her pupils who brought a book to school. While his classmates were at the public library, searching for worthy volumes for Miss Morgan, Ginsberg happened to discover that there were thousands of books in his father's house. He began by bringing one of them to school each morning, but soon, inspired by the rapid accumulation of stars on his report card, Ginsberg was coming to school with two, then five, then ten. "There were books I'd read, books I hadn't read, books I'd looked at a little, books with all the dope on the jackets," Ginsberg says. "And the funny thing was that instead of saying this was unfair, Miss Morgan would encourage it. Which was very groovy. So I got very good marks and kept on carrying these big loads of books to school in my red cart and showing them off, and Miss Morgan would say 'Wonderful!' She said it was like an indication of how involved in letters I was."

One night after a reading in New Jersey, Ginsberg ran into an old classmate of his from grammar school. They recognized each other immediately, and spent quite a few minutes remarking on how little either of them had changed. Then the man, who was now a lawyer, asked Ginsberg if he remembered Miss Morgan.

"Miss Morgan, she was the greatest," the man said.

Ginsberg nodded solemnly. "Miss Morgan gave me my start in literature," he said.

Ginsberg came home to Paterson as soon as the Psychiatric Institute would let him go. He and Solomon had spent a good deal of time there composing madhouse letters, which they never had the heart to mail, to a long list of famous people on the outside. William Carlos Williams was one of them—Solomon preferred writing to Harry Truman and T. S. Eliot—and when he got home, Ginsberg persuaded one of the local papers to send him to Dr. Williams' on an interview. "I was too shy just to see him as a poet, so I went as a kind of humble newsman," Ginsberg says. "We had a lovely conversation, and I began sending him poems and letters about Céline and Burroughs and Kerouac, and all the different influences I was interested in. It was sort of like a big responsibility for Williams—my being a younger poet from Paterson. We'd take walks occasionally. He'd show me his Paterson, and I'd show him mine—I'd show him what *my* epiphanous places were. Places like by the river, under the bridge, where I masturbated for the first time. Where I kissed that girl who moved away. Where I saw a gang fight. Where I always felt ashamed for some reason. The hedge where I was lonely. And I showed him the library, where I first read Dostoevski. So that while there was like a whole other scene going in New York—around the Cedar Bar and the San Remo, where all the writers and the abstract expressionists and the musicians were hanging out—which was like a big new influence on me, there was also Williams in Paterson, talking about native ground."

Ginsberg worked hard on his Paterson explorations, and most of the poems in his earliest collection, *Empty Mirror*, were written during the year he spent at home. One of them, "How Come He Got Canned at the Ribbon Factory," was about his first Paterson job—Ginsberg lasted two weeks, due in part to his own failure to master the art of tying together broken ribbon threads in five seconds while racing a conveyor belt, and in part to the general reluctance of the ladies on his assembly line, who were not happy with the competition, to tie his threads for him. His next job involved three months as a hack on the local house organ of the American Federation of Labor. It lasted until Ginsberg announced a plan he had to investigate the New Jersey Mafia's union control.

That year, Ginsberg lived with his father and his new stepmother. His own mother, Naomi Ginsberg, had been mad since Ginsberg was a boy, and his father, Louis, who for some years had been living all alone in a small apartment, finally had remarried and moved to a roomy two-family house. Ginsberg took over the basement, which was duly papered with a Chinese calligraphic print that he had spotted in a Paterson wallpaper store. He still keeps most of his books and papers in his old basement retreat. No one in the family would consider repapering it.

"That time in Paterson was, for me, like the renunciation of an obsessional search for the circumstances of some visionary cosmic consciousness, like the acceptance of what was real, of the world as world, absolute as it is," Ginsberg says. He likes to quote Williams, on a walk there, telling him, "The sea is not our home," just as he likes to quote Martin Buber, years later in Jerusalem, saying "Mark my words, young man, one day you will remember that it's a *human* universe we live in." The image of an empty mirror, Ginsberg says, was his image for the defeat of visionary, metaphysical strivings (an empty mirror is also a Buddhist metaphor), and his poem "The Shrouded Stranger," from which he took the image for his title, has a part that goes:

> I dreamed I was dreaming again
> and decided to go down the years
> looking for the Shrouded Stranger.
> I knew the old bastard
> was hanging around somewhere.
>
> I couldn't find him for a while,
> went looking under beds,
> pulling mattresses off,
> and finally discovered him
> hiding under the springs
> crouched in the corner:
>
> met him face to face at last.
> I didn't even recognize him.
> "I'll bet you didn't think
> it was me after all," he said.

While Williams was leading Ginsberg back to his beginnings in New Jersey, Kerouac, in New York, had started writing *On the Road*. He had been inspired by a forty-page sentence in a letter from Neal Cassady, and, sitting down one day with a huge Teletype roll tucked into his typewriter, he began with the first thought he happened to have and kept on typing until, three weeks later, he came to the end of the roll. "I was lagging behind, and it was Jack's explosion of energy and composition

that really turned me on to writing," Ginsberg says. "Like, he'd
discovered a whole world of composition and rhythm—the rhythm
of long sentences paralleling, sort of, some of the great tenor
saxophones. Sentences like Charlie Parker and Lester Young. It
was a kind of swim in the great sea of prose. Kind of Proustian,
actually, like Peter driving—Peter, who, in a sense, has always
been a specialist in simultaneous perceptions and seems to be
able to drive and conduct a conversation with six or seven people
at once and at the same time notice everything and take
care of all the little details in the car. Jack's sentences were
unstructured, in the sense of like there being no single purpose
to them. But they were structured to the actual situation, which
is something *really* important. Something that emerged in art
later on as collage, and then as light shows. Something that
emerged in psychology as the kind of rapport necessary for communication with schizophrenics. And emerged in LSD, with the
undifferentiated consciousness which notices everything at once
and doesn't discriminate between what's more important and
what's less. And there I'd been, trying to write little simple poems
like Williams—and, actually, still writing like Sir Thomas Wyatt
in my secret heart."

Ginsberg says that the next few years were like a gathering of
forces, a kind of literary *Walpurgisnacht* when all the experiences
of the generation—"All the jails and the sufferings and the
deaths and suicides and the flip-outs and the radiances and
the peyote visions, and also the Blake visions, and everybody
rushing up and down the country," he says—were finally arrayed.
One by one, his friends began drifting back to New York, and
Ginsberg himself moved back when he met a girl who worked
for the National Community Research Center and had found
a job for him. Kerouac got married again. Huncke was out of jail
for a while. And Burroughs, who had been writing the first draft
of *Junkie* as a series of letters to Ginsberg, arrived from Mexico.
(Joan Burroughs died in Mexico. At a party there one night, she
demanded that Burroughs shoot a glass of vodka off her head.

Burroughs misfired. When he came to New York, he had just been tried and acquitted on a manslaughter charge.) Ginsberg took an apartment with Burroughs on Seventh Street, and they apparently played out the end of their old affair with considerable literary gain and an equal amount of trauma on both sides. He says that he was a little frightened, at times, by Burroughs, a sardonic comrade who, according to Ginsberg, "kept insisting that the two us were ultimately going to schlup together, sort of schlup and absorb each other, a kind of monstrous junkie-organic-protoplasmic schlup of two beings craving the other half of their souls." (Ginsberg has never quite managed to figure out what exactly Burroughs meant by "schlup.") At any rate, shortly after Ginsberg left for California, Burroughs moved to Tangier.

Corso turned up late in 1950 to complete the scene whose compound message Ginsberg was to carry to the West Coast. They met by chance, in a downtown bar called the Pony Stable, a few months after Corso finished a prison stretch for stealing a radio. He had been born in the Village, above a mortuary near the San Remo, and Ginsberg says that at seventeen Corso was a cross between a lone, natural, jail poet, like Genet, and a lyric poet, "very deep in his Italian-Greenwich Village roots." After they exchanged some poems that night at the Pony Stable, Corso confessed that he had fallen in love with a very beautiful lady who lived across the street from his furnished room. Every night for a month now, he had been peeping courteously from his window while the lady undressed and performed sexy and complicated dances at a large mirror, and Corso was so proud of her talent that he invited Ginsberg over for a peep, too. Standing at the window, a little while later, Ginsberg was startled to discover that Corso's lady was one of his own girl friends, an outgoing soul from Lusk, Wyoming, who was making her way in New York. He and Corso crossed the street immediately, and their literary friendship, Ginsberg says, began.

For the next two years Ginsberg moved in and out of the market-research business, did a stint as a copy boy at the old

World Telegram ("Actually, I have a good background in the underbelly of mass communications," was what he once told a reporter who had called him a beat public-relations man), practiced poetry under the combined, if advertantly so, tutelage of Williams, Burroughs, Kerouac, and Corso, and raced around town trying to publish books by all his friends. He worshiped his writing friends, with some of the same blanket enthusiasm Miss Morgan had for books, and anyone asking Ginsberg then—and now—about his own work was likely to get a long and rapturous reply on the virtues of the whole group. No doubt some of this enthusiasm came from the fact that the beats, together, were breaking through the "syndrome of shutdown" Ginsberg talks about, and that this breaking-through-together was, very likely, something that none of them could have managed alone. His friends themselves say that Ginsberg's feeling for their accomplishments was just the literary side of the poet's doggedly rosy point of view on all of his old heroes and amours.

Solomon, who was out of the hospital by now, was Ginsberg's introduction to publishing. One of Solomon's uncles owned a paperback house—his other two uncles, whom Ginsberg found far more interesting, were a master Bronx bookmaker and Rudolf Hally, the old Liberal Party candidate for mayor—and when Solomon went to work there as a reader, all of *his* friends began sending manuscripts to him. Ginsberg sent *Junkie*, which the house, Ace Books, brought out as an archetypally cheap thriller, complete with a cover picture of a woman in whorehouse red sticking a needle into her arm, while several murderous-looking types watched from a fire escape (there were no women in *Junkie*, with the exception of Burroughs' wife) and a rash of quasi-scientific footnotes disclaiming the author's statements about drugs. Burroughs, who was an heir to the Burroughs' Corporation and on a kind of permanent remittance from his parents in Palm Beach, got eight hundred dollars for the book as an advance on royalties.

Having dispensed with *Junkie*, Ginsberg began carrying *On the*

Road around. (Ginsberg left his own poetry to Williams, who wrote a fine introduction to *Empty Mirror* and tried, for a while, to get somebody to publish it; the book finally came out in 1961, six years after Ferlinghetti published *Howl* and the same year that *Kaddish* appeared.) Harcourt, Brace and Company, which published *The Town and the City*, Kerouac's first novel, had apparently just rejected *On the Road* as "awful." The Bobbs-Merrill Company, where Ginsberg left it, turned it down as "boring," but the editors at Ace, who were evidently confused by Kerouac's long-breath sentences and who told Ginsberg that the book was "unintelligible," gave Kerouac an advance to write something else in a nice, lurid, narrative style. Kerouac started working on a long book, which he has never published, called *Visions of Cody*. It began as a narrative, but after about eighty pages, turned into an experiment in tape transcriptions, pure sounds, and improvisations on the original text. Ginsberg called it "spontaneous bop prosody."

"What happened to me," Ginsberg says, "was like suddenly being hit with Kerouac's idea that once you wrote something you couldn't really change it, because that was the manifestation of the mind's moving in time and the attempt to change and revise and restructure and reorient was, in a sense, a lie. Or a covering. A *thought* covering. Like what was necessary really was to trust and depend on the mind itself to swim free to the other shore. And the other thing was to speak now and forever hold your piece—like to give cleanness to writing in the moment of eternity you had to realize that the feeling of writing was forever and could never be changed, rather than to try to reverse, go back, change it, cut it up. Like you had to go forward in time in your writing. Always. No revise, *re*vision. You had to stick to the primary vision."

Since then, Ginsberg has rarely thrown a word away. His composition-book jottings (the books are carefully labeled with his name and address, and signed with a Buddha fish print and the message, "Please return, in the name of *Hare Krishna!*") are all stored in his apartment and in the basement of his father's house, and so is every one of his letters which managed, in the course of its composition, to turn into a relatively worthy piece of prose. He saves copies of all his interviews, which he has come to consider a sort of supplementary spoken-word output, as well as his various manifestos, journals, and diaries. And his editing, when any of them are published, consists mainly in correcting his spelling, which is often dreadful, filling in the names of forgotten deities, holy men, and colleagues, and, in general, transfering scribbles onto some semblance of a legible page. He edits his poetry—even his talked-into-the-tape-recorder poetry—in very much the same way. Whether poetry like this will stand up critically is, by now, almost beside the point to Ginsberg. He says that he looks at his writing the way he looks at all his behavior—as gestures of a friendly, literary being with a particular urge to communicate himself.

One night in the winter of 1967, Ginsberg and Basil Bunting, the Northumberland poet, were driving south on Broadway with a few of their friends. Bunting, who had read that night at the Guggenheim Museum, was peering out of the side window of the car, while Ginsberg, in the back seat, delivered a running monologue on some of the groovier changes in New York. Bunting had not been in the city for over thirty years, and Ginsberg was determined to show him around. He had just spirited Bunting out of a dull literary party on Morningside Drive, but now, on their way downtown for a look at one of Ginsberg's favorite hangouts, Bunting suddenly begged off the visit and asked to be dropped at his hotel.

Bunting was yawning. He was in his sixties—a slight, shy grandfather, with hair the color of coarse-ground pepper and a pair of lively and remarkably pointed eyebrows of a sort that are often associated with wise and witty elder poets but, in fact, are very rarely seen on anyone. Earlier, at the Guggenheim, Bunting had staged his reading after the performances of the classical poets of Persia, where he had lived in the forties as a correspondent for the *London Times,* and he had enlisted Ginsberg's help in finding a beautiful young saki to sit on a pillow at his feet and pour wine for him. Ginsberg's friendly, empathetic jitters had amused him—Ginsberg raced around the auditorium, trying to locate a suitable virgin from among all the sleek literary ladies who were in the audience—and he chuckled now at Ginsberg's insistence that they hit a place called Max's Kansas City "to see what was happening."

"Come on, Basil, you should be celebrating," Ginsberg said, leaning forward, on his elbows, so that his beard dipped over into the front seat. "Parts of the poem were really groovy. The part about gossamer hair. The hair brushing the cheek. The spider web." He was talking about *Brigg Flats,* Bunting's long autobiographical poem, and he repeated the lines he liked with a particular pleasure in his voice. Ginsberg considered Bunting the finest living English poet.

"I don't know." Bunting sighed a little. "The death part was not at all as powerful at this reading as it's been before. I think one needs a smaller group—something intimate—for a poem like that."

"I tried to write a poem like you once," Ginsberg said. "The one about Piccadilly. I set it up for myself like kind of an exercise. I said, like, 'How would Basil write this poem?' and then I went ahead. Like I revised and revised. It ended up pretty rigid and condensed." Ginsberg laughed. "That kind of writing's not my scene—I haven't got the strength," he said.

"I know that poem," Bunting said. "I thought it was rather good, myself."

Ginsberg shook his head. "Did you have to work on it much? *Brigg Flats?*" he said finally.

"Years." Bunting smiled. "I started out with twenty-five thousand lines and pared it down to seven hundred and fifty. I believe I threw the rest away."

"Wasn't there anything of interest to you in all those lines? Like maybe *revealing* of you?" Ginsberg said.

Bunting looked at him. "Good God, no," he said. "All I wanted to salvage were the *good* lines."

Ginsberg sat back for a minute, thinking. "I suppose that makes you more human—all those corrections," he said, with a grin. "Like it shows that you're not some superior being, some perfect being. Still—twenty-five thousand lines *lost*. Couldn't you have just *saved* them? Maybe like publish them as 'Work in Progress.' Or give them to a library for future Bunting scholars to fool around with."

"Oh dear, no," Bunting said, sounding embarrassed. "I don't go in for that sort of literary revelation. I throw away *everything*. I was cleaning house a few years back, and there were over a hundred letters from Pound that I threw away."

Ginsberg groaned. "Don't you think some people might have been interested? Not necessarily *you*—but *some* people?"

"I'm afraid it's just that I don't find myself very interesting," Bunting said.

"Maybe not *you*, but Pound is certainly interesting," Ginsberg said, laughing. "Anyway, Basil, some people might find you interesting. *I* find you interesting."

"Ah, but of what use are letters like that?" Bunting said. "The only use for letters nowadays seems to be to sell them for a great deal of money to someplace like the University of Texas."

"You see, Basil, you missed out on the big money," Ginsberg said, leaning forward to give Bunting a hug. They were at Times Square now, and Ginsberg, noticing *Le Chien d'Andalou* billed on a nudie marquee, had just rolled down his window and poked out his head for a better look. His head, at the moment, was wrapped in a six-foot crimson-and-white scarf from the Harvard Co-op. When Bunting remarked that he found New York a trifle chilly after Santa Barbara, where he was teaching for the year, Ginsberg said that, what with his scarf and all his hair, he was always able to keep warm. They talked for a minute about the movie and about some of the new underground movies that Ginsberg wanted Bunting to see, and then Ginsberg said, suddenly, "Come on, Basil, how can you say that those letters are useless? Like maybe a dozen people in the world would be able to, like, experience some big alteration of consciousness from them. Even if it's *one* person, they're worth it."

Bunting shook his head. "I'm afraid I just don't go in for that sort of gossip," he said.

"But you and Pound," Ginsberg cut in. "Those times in Paris and Rapallo. A record of that scene would be *useful*. Hey, maybe you should write a little something now—"

"No, no—that sort of thing doesn't last," Bunting said. "And I'm not interested in it for poetry."

"I am," Ginsberg said. "More and more. Like I'm beginning to see my poetry as a kind of record of the times—my impressions of what's going on, like what's going on in terms of how my being responds to it. I don't know. It may not last, but I think it's maybe useful in that it helps clarify the present. Like what I did last year was put a long poem on tape, in the car, going back and forth across the country."

"But that's it," Bunting said. "I can't help feeling that a record of my life in those terms would not be very interesting." He took a long puff on a cigarette that Ginsberg had lit and handed him. "I'd actually be happy if *nothing* remained of my life after I died."

"Not even the poems?" Ginsberg said.

Bunting smiled. "Why not? As I say—and you are kind enough to argue—I just don't happen to find myself particularly interesting."

"Aha," Ginsberg said, laughing. "Here all along I thought you were destroying everything because of some perfect, objective, *hard* principle—like you were saying, 'Let nothing remain but the works themselves'—and here it's really because you think that you're not interesting. It's just some big ego problem. What kind of objectivity is that?"

Bunting laughed too. They had turned on Twenty-third Street and were double-parked in front of the Chelsea Hotel. Ginsberg tried one last time to coax his friend into a trip to the Kansas City, but Bunting said that he was off to the Harvard *Advocate* for a reading early in the morning, and needed to get some sleep.

"We were there once—Peter and Gregory and me," Ginsberg said. "They're all right. Like Eliott wrote for them."

Bunting sighed. "Knowing students, I shall have to talk for eighteen hours a day and drink for fourteen," he said.

"Ask them for pot, it's easier on the constitution," Ginsberg suggested. Then he said, "Hey, that's the other thing I did this year—I became a Sivaist. Like now I'm an official worshiper of the god of pot."

"So now you're on your way to the poet's heaven." Bunting chuckled.

"No, I'm probably on my way to court," Ginsberg said.

Chapter 2

On a snowy Sunday morning in Paterson, Allen Ginsberg and his father settled into a pair of plumped chintz armchairs in Mr. Ginsberg's living room to look at the *New York Times* together and talk over the schedule for a father-and-son poetry reading that they were going to give that night at Paterson State. Ginsberg's stepmother, Edith, was in the kitchen fixing a big breakfast of bagels, bialys, lox, cream cheese, and scrambled eggs, and Maretta, who had come home with Ginsberg for the weekend, was still asleep. It was Ginsberg's first visit to the house since early fall, when a warrant had been issued in Paterson for his arrest on a marijuana charge. The mayor of Paterson, who was on his way out of office, had ordered the arrest after Ginsberg informed the audience at another family reading, at the local Young Men's Hebrew Association, that he had "heightened the experience" of a poetic pilgrimage that morning with his father to the Passaic Falls. Paterson's policemen had thereupon combed the city for Ginsberg, who had last been seen carrying his purple woven book bag and wearing horn-rimmed glasses, his tan hiking boots, rumpled khaki pants, his unmatching gray socks, a relatively threadbare brown tweed jacket, an old white button-down, finger cymbals, and an oracle's ring, and after a few days they located a likely-looking beard near a bar downtown. By the time the gentleman with the beard was released as a sartorial follower of Ginsberg, but by no means the genuine poetic article, Ginsberg was safely across the state line in New York. He thought about returning to Paterson, with a phalanx of reporters, to be arrested publicly as a first move in a marijuana-law test case, but he abandoned the scheme as "too embarrassing" to his father, and left for the West Coast, to teach at Berkeley, instead. While Ginsberg was away, a new and friendlier mayor took office, and when he finally came home, a few weeks ago, the case against him was dismissed, on the ground of insufficient evidence, by the Paterson Municipal Court.

Ginsberg's five months as the poet who was "wanted in Paterson" reminded him of one of the letters he had written to William Carlos Williams, from San Francisco, over ten years ago:

> . . . I have NOT absconded from Paterson. I do have a whitmanic mania & nostalgia for cities and detail & panorama and isolation in jungle and pole, like the images you pick up. When I've seen enough I'll be back to splash in the Passaic again only with a body so naked and happy City Hall will have to call out the Riot Spad. When I come back I'll make big political speeches in the mayoralty campaign like I did when I was 16 only this time I'll have W. C. Fields on my left and Jehovah on my right. Why not? Paterson is only a big sad poppa who needs compassion . . . In any case Beauty is where I hang my hat. And reality. And America . . . I mean to say Paterson is not a task like Milton going down to hell, it's a flower to the mind too . . .

He mentioned the letter to his father, who was peering at him over the top of the "News of the Week in Review." Mr. Ginsberg said that he remembered it. At seventy-one, Louis Ginsberg was compact and jaunty, with quizzical, popping eyes, a scrubbed-to-gleaming forehead, and a favorite expression of slightly oppressed seniority. For forty years he had taught English in the Paterson public high schools, and for fifty he had been writing and steadily publishing lyric poems. At the moment he was stagestruck, according to Mrs. Ginsberg, who dated this new passion of her husband's from the night of the first Ginsberg reading, *père et fils*, in March of 1966.

"You *did* bring home some good clothes for the reading tonight, didn't you, Allen?" Mr. Ginsberg, who was already dressed for the event in a new polka-dot bow tie and a blue-serge suit, asked his son.

Ginsberg looked up from Section I, which he was scouring for hippie news, and laughed. "Yeah, I've got *my* suit, too," he said.

Mr. Ginsberg sighed. "We'll show them that the Ginsberg names means poetry," he said, and he added, philosophically, "You know, Allen, you're popular with the college crowd, but with a real audience you need me for balance. I'm like the stamp to your letter."

Ginsberg shook his head.

"I told you that one," Mr. Ginsberg said. "The one where the stamp says to the letter, 'I may be square, but I send you.'"

Ginsberg groaned.

His father, who had long been known in the Passaic County press as "the Paterson pun-dit" or, alternatively, "the Paterson punny man," went on to say that he had just recatalogued his pun collection by subjects, such as "Flirtation," "Love," "Automobiles," and "Alcoholics," and now had a comprehensive folder just on beatniks. He stood up to get it from his desk, in the sunroom, but Ginsberg waved him down.

"You know, Louis, I think you secretly dig my poetry," Ginsberg said.

Louis Ginsberg shrugged. "You're a new generation, Allen,"

he said. "I believe in poetic coexistence, but you young people —you don't like a nice, regular, flexible meter. You don't like discipline. You don't like rhyme. You say it's not natural. I ask you, what could be more natural than rhyme? Rhymes are so enchanting, so instinctive. Children make rhymes as soon as they can speak." Mr. Ginsberg sighed again, and went right on. "And you've got such new mores. For instance, you use four-letter words that I was brought up not to use in company. And the way you live. You don't have to live like that, Allen. You're a world-famous poet."

Ginsberg made a mudra to assure his father that he recognized and respected the soul of another sentient being in the living room. Then he said "Om," signifying the ultimate oneness of all views.

"And these odd religions," Mr. Ginsberg said. He seemed to be warming to the chance at hand, and Ginsberg chuckled, listening to him. In December, he had taken his father to a birthday party for his friend Swami Satchidananda, the Hindu yoga and holy man who lived on West End Avenue. Mr. Ginsberg had had indigestion after three spoonfuls of the Swami's party food, and had ever since displayed a certain impatience with the customs of the East.

"I bet it was that curry, Louis," Ginsberg said.

Mr. Ginsberg shook his head. He said it was really Maretta that was bothering him. She had arrived at the house last night with a sack of equipment for her rather unnerving meditations —a tattered paperback copy of the *Tibetan Book of the Dead*, a pair of finger cymbals, Ginsberg's big metal dorje, her own faceted gazing crystal, and a packet of incense sticks—and had emptied it out on the living-room couch for the Ginsbergs to see. Then, just before bed, she had informed Mr. Ginsberg that her sadhana was hashish. "What's with this Maretta?" Mr. Ginsberg asked. "Why can't you bring home a nice Jewish girl?"

Ginsberg, laughing, threw up his hands. "For the love of God, Louis," he said, "here for years you've been saying, 'Please, just bring home a *girl* for a change,' and now that I do, you want a *Jewish* one?"

"You're such an *experimenter*, Allen," Mr. Ginsberg said. "Tibetan Buddhist girl friends. Swamis. Drugs. All this talk from you about pot—'It's so elevating, Louis. So ecstatic. My soul is outside my body. I see ultimate reality.'" Mr. Ginsberg frowned. "You know what *I* say? I say, 'Allen, take it easy.'"

Ginsberg, who had removed his shoes and was sitting in the lotus position in the chintz chair, leaned forward and took his father's hand. "*You* should take it easy, Louis," he said. "You'll wear yourself out straightening me out."

"Look, Allen, it's been a long time since I've been able to get you to the old homestead," Mr. Ginsberg said. "Your father waits, counts the days."

"Well, the troubles are over now," Ginsberg said. "Was it bad for you here? With the trial?"

Mr. Ginsberg shook his head. "You know, some people talk," he said. "You hear all sorts of odd things." He shuffled through a pile of papers on an end table by his chair and handed a clipping to Ginsberg. It was a letter to the editor of the Paterson *Call*: "In reference to Allen Ginsberg, whom your reporter, George James, described as a poet, living legend, and international traveler. So what! I was extremely disgusted with your paper's continuously shielding and glorifying this poet. One would think that you were trying to defend a moral saintly man instead of a person who openly admitted that he was smoking marijuana, which is unlawful . . . I was a student at Central High School and remember his father, Louis Ginsberg, who taught there. Being a parent myself I do not condemn him because of his son, but I am shocked that he has joined his son as a team in the poetry readings. It seems that he must certainly enjoy all this publicity, despite what kind it may be . . ."

Ginsberg tossed the clipping back on the table.

"Some people are like that," Mr. Ginsberg said. "I've got no axiom to grind."

"I was just wondering what the gossip in the coffee shops was, that's all," Ginsberg said.

"Allen, I *told* you," Mr. Ginsberg said. "Everybody thought that it was pretty silly of the previous mayor to make a fuss. That the evidence was flimsy. Everybody's glad it turned out fine. Still . . ." Mr. Ginsberg looked up.

"Go ahead," Ginsberg said.

"Well, *my* feeling," Mr. Ginsberg said, "is really that you should obey the law, and then when the law is changed, you can go ahead and smoke all you want."

Maretta walked into the living room, yawning.

"I felt I didn't need the drugs," Mr. Ginsberg told her. "I felt that with my *own* imagination I could receive the majesty and grandeur of the Falls."

Maretta nodded, and began poking her hair into a new fringed shawl which she had wrapped around her head. She was dressed for breakfast in baggy black ski pants and purple sari cloth. The dorje and the crystal were both on strings around her neck. Mr. Ginsberg stared, speechless, as she arranged herself on his brown-slipcovered couch.

"Well, young lady, how do you like it here?" Mr. Ginsberg asked, finally, with a sweep of his hand.

Maretta contemplated the small, tidy living room. It was painted a rosy tan and had beige carpeting and silvery nylon curtains at the windows. There were urns of bright green plastic leaves in a fireplace at one end and, at the other, a gilded white secretary and an enormous television set. Photographs of various Ginsberg grandchildren were displayed along the walls, and above the brown couch there were two Montmartre flower market scenes, which Mr. Ginsberg pointed to proudly, telling Maretta that he had picked them out himself.

Maretta, however, was busy scrutinizing a lampshade through her crystal bead.

"I imagine you're meditating," Mr. Ginsberg said, finally. "Do you meditate often?"

"I've sat in a few caves," Maretta said.

"And have you been grazing and ciphering ancient Buddhist texts?" Mr. Ginsberg went on. "Are you wiser now than before?"

"Yeah," Maretta said.

Mr. Ginsberg put down his paper. "With you young people," he said, "it's like the one about children—you can love them in the abstract, but it's hard in the concrete."

"Maretta speaks Tibetan," Ginsberg said.

"So what's wrong with English?" Mr. Ginsberg said.

Mrs. Ginsberg, who had come to the door, called them in to breakfast. She had been watching Maretta and the two men with a certain amount of motherly amusement. When she married Louis Ginsberg, in 1950, she had already raised a family of her own. Some of the grandchildren on the wall were hers, and Ginsberg began asking after them as they walked into a bright pink kitchen, off the living room, where a round Formica table was heaped with Sunday-morning delicatessen food. Then he announced that he was starving.

Maretta asked if there were any crackers around.

"I was telling Allen," Mr. Ginsberg said when they were all sitting at the table, "how his old man in the suburbs waits and waits for him."

Mrs. Ginsberg, who was a good-looking woman with fluffy gray hair, passed him a bagel. "Your father is full of baloney, Allen," she said, laughing.

Ginsberg, who was tackling a bialy spread with cream cheese and strawberry jam, glanced at his father.

"Well, what have you been doing, Allen?" Mr. Ginsberg said. "How was Berkeley? You know, there weren't too many letters from you this time. Time was, you'd go on a trip, you used to send long letters to your father. 'Louis, tell me, what is life? Who *am* I?' Which reminds me of what Thomas Mann once said: 'Is life worth living? It depends on the liver.' " He turned to Maretta and added, "I've got all the letters down in the basement, if you'd like to see them sometime."

"Beautiful," Maretta said.

"Yes, they were," Mr. Ginsberg said. "Allen used to be very philosophical."

Ginsberg, heading toward the stove for some scrambled eggs, called out that California had been groovy. "I bought some land there," he said. "Sierra land."

"What's wrong with land near here?" Mr. Ginsberg said.

"I'm going to buy some land here *too*," Ginsberg said. "Maybe a farm in New Jersey or New York—some place to get away to."

"We're going to have a plutocrat in the family," Mrs. Ginsberg said proudly.

Mr. Ginsberg pointed to his son at the stove. "Shall I tell him, Edith?" he said.

Mrs. Ginsberg nodded.

"Edith and I are going to Europe," Mr. Ginsberg said.

"Hey, that's groovy," Ginsberg said, running over to slap his father on the back. He told Maretta that it was his parents' first trip abroad.

"It's for two weeks, in September," Mr. Ginsberg went on. "It can't be longer, because I'm going to be teaching night school at Rutgers again. Composition and modern American poetry." He leaned toward Maretta and whispered, "My students there, they ask me about my poetry, so I tell them that my son's a poet, and then that way they learn about Allen, too."

"Make it August," Ginsberg cut in. "*I'll* be in Europe in August."

"Prices are awfully high then," Mrs. Ginsberg said.

"But you'll stay with *me*," Ginsberg said. "I have some groovy friends in Europe. There's a literary lady in London with like a huge mansion in Belgravia and a salon and all sorts of fascinating cats running around. Then there's a Rothschild kid I know in Italy—"

"Should we go alone, do you think, or on a guided tour?" Mr. Ginsberg broke in.

"Man, you don't want to go on any tour," Maretta said, looking stunned. "*I* hitchhike."

"I don't want you to worry about *anything*," Ginsberg went on. "I'll get your rooms. Show you around. It'll be a ball, going around Europe with you. Think of Paris."

"I don't know, Allen," Mr. Ginsberg said. "Paris with you? The old gray mare might not be up to it."

Ginsberg chuckled. "Come on, Louis," he said. "We'll get rid of Edith. I'll take you to all the whorehouses."

"One stipulation," Mrs. Ginsberg said, pouring coffee. "I get to go shopping."

"And all the bordellos," Ginsberg said. "All the hashish points. All the big scary Arab *couscous* cellars."

"I'm afraid I'll fall asleep, like at that Swami character's," Mr. Ginsberg said.

"Well, *one* thing's definite," Ginsberg went on. "In Paris, I turn you on to pot."

Maretta nodded enthusiastically.

Mr. Ginsberg patted Maretta's hand. "Well, young lady, who knows? It might turn me on to whole new endeavors," he said.

"Right," Ginsberg said. "First, we'll sit around high, reading Apollinaire, and *then* we'll make a big pilgrimage to Shelley's grave."

"Listen, Allen, I have a lot of work to do when I get home," Mr. Ginsberg interrupted. "I have my abstracts to revise."

"Man, *what* are abstracts?" Maretta said.

Mr. Ginsberg explained. He said that whenever he read a book he took notes on it, and then he wrote an abstract of the book from them. "And whenever the abstracts pile up, like now, I compile *quintessences* of the abstracts," he said.

Maretta appeared to be confused.

"It's like this," Mr. Ginsberg said. "Right now I'm swamped with abstracts and way behind on quintessences."

Ginsberg said, "*Om.*"

Mrs. Ginsberg stood up and smoothed down the skirt of her bright blue knitted dress. She was going back to the delicatessen, she said, to pick up food for a party before the reading that night.

Ginsberg stood up, too, looking a little alarmed. "You don't have to make a big deal just for me," he said.

"Oh, it's nothing," Mrs. Ginsberg said. "Just the family and friends. The Cohens, from Bradley Beach. The Gorlins, from Rumson. You can't not feed them when they come all that way."

"Peace. You're right," Ginsberg said. "It'll be groovy." He walked Mrs. Ginsberg to the back door and stood there for a minute to look at his father's rose garden, which was covered with fresh snow.

Mr. Ginsberg stayed at the table and began telling Maretta stories about Ginsberg as a boy. "One time," Mr. Ginsberg said, "when Allen was in college, a friend told me that Allen had written a poem that was going to be in the Columbia paper. So I called him up. 'Why didn't you tell me?' I asked him. And you know what Allen said?"

Maretta shook her head.

"He said, 'Louis, I thought you didn't *want* me to write poetry.'"

"I don't remember that story," Ginsberg said, sitting down and pouring himself another cup of coffee. "What *I* remember is that once you introduced me and my brother to some friend and you said, 'Eugene and I, we write poems, but Allen —he's normal.'"

"You think I was being very serious?" Mr. Ginsberg asked, with a big grin.

"You mean you *weren't?*" Ginsberg said.

Chapter 3

It was a gloomy day for the Establishment when Ginsberg and his friends announced their arrival on the literary scene. There was a pall in the hearts of critics and an icy silence in the offices of reigning publishers which had not been matched since Whitman went whooping through New Jersey, a hundred years earlier. Freshman English instructors watched their charges for slips of enthusiasm. Mothers rushed their sons to the tailor to avert disaster. And the aficionados of bohemia prepared for their first ripe literary scandal since Molly Bloom rode Blazes Boylan around her front room. The beats, according to all the rumors, were a mad amalgam of everything unpleasant from *Les Miserables* to "Les Fauves."

The Six Gallery reading was a good beginning for Ginsberg, and for a while after it, he says, he was happy and oblivious, playing in his garden at Berkeley and sitting at his desk in San Francisco writing poems. News of a poets' community was bringing young writers from all over the country out to the West Coast. Robert Creeley, who had already published the work of the new Eastern poets in *Black Mountain Review*, had come to San Francisco for a visit with Kerouac and Ginsberg and had stayed to put together *Black Mountain #7*, which turned out to be a classic of the movement, with writing by Ginsberg, Corso, Kerouac, Burroughs, Snyder, Duncan, Philip Whalen, Philip Lamantia, Louis Zukofsky, Hubert Selby, Jr., and Denise Levertov. Then, when money problems forced the shutdown of the experimental Black Mountain College, most of Creeley's students followed him. Finally, Corso arrived from Cambridge, where he had been living under the combined auspices of a girl friend at Radcliffe and several admiring Harvard undergraduates, who, in due time, put out their own San Francisco poetry issue of the *Cambridge Review*.

Ferlinghetti published *Howl and Other Poems* in October of 1956. And, as Ginsberg had hoped, William Carlos Williams wrote the introduction:

> When he was younger, and I was younger, I used to know Allen Ginsberg, a young poet living in Paterson, New Jersey, where he, son of a well-known poet, had been born and grew up. He was physically slight of build and mentally much disturbed by the life which he had encountered about him during those first years after the First World War as it was exhibited to him in and about New York City. He was always on the point of "going away," where it didn't seem to matter; he disturbed me, I never thought he'd live to grow up and write a book of poems. His ability to survive, travel, and go on writing astonished me. That he has gone on developing and perfecting his art is not less amazing to me.
>
> Now he turns up fifteen or twenty years later with an arresting poem. Literally he has, from all the evidence, been through hell. On the way he met a man named Carl Solomon, with whom he shared among the teeth and excrement of this life something that cannot be described but in the words he has

used to describe it. It is a howl of defeat. Not defeat at all, for he has gone through defeat as if it were an ordinary experience, a trivial experience. Everyone in this life is defeated, but a man, if he be a man, is not defeated.

*   *   *

It is the belief in the art of poetry that has gone hand in hand with this man into his Golgotha, from that charnel house, similar, in every way, to that of the Jews in the past war. But this is in our own country, our own fondest purlieus. We are blind and live our blind lives out in blindness. Poets are damned but they are not blind, they see with the eyes of the angels. This poet sees through and all around the horrors he partakes of in the very intimate details of his poem. He avoids nothing but experiences it to the hilt. He contains it. Claims it as his own—and, we believe, laughs at it and has the time and effrontery to love a fellow of his choice and record that love in a well-made poem.

Hold back the edges of your gowns, Ladies, we are going through hell.

By the time Ferlinghetti was arrested, a few months after publication, on charges that *Howl* violated the California obscenity code, the book had sold out its first printing and thousands of typed-up copies were circulating through the poetry underground. Three more printings had gone to press by the end of a trial that made the beats—and Ginsberg in particular—a subject of rabid controversy in households where no one had ever met a beatnik, much less glanced at the offending poem. (Today, *Howl* has been translated, officially, into French, German, Spanish, Italian, Czech, Russian, Bengali, Hindi, and Japanese, and run off mimeograph machines and stencilers in contraband editions in at least a dozen other languages; there were 106,000 copies of the American edition in print when the book went into its seventeenth printing in September, 1966).

All the attention the beats were getting drove the critics into tantrums. Richard Eberhart, the poet, had written a long essay on the poetry renaissance for the *New York Times*, and his article, along with Ferlinghetti's trial, started most of the publicity. It was a friendly, noncommittal piece, but it turned out to be the last kind word about the new poets in the respectable press for years. Rexroth, who had introduced the happy apocalypse at the Six Gallery, was by now embroiled in a war of grudges and hurt feelings between the younger poets in North Beach and Berkeley and the older writers, like himself, who, not without some justice, complained that Ginsberg and his friends were stealing their scene on their own home ground. Rexroth's particular disenchantment, according to Ginsberg, was somewhat speeded by the fact that he lost a girl friend to Creeley shortly after the Black Mountain poet arrived. Whatever the reason, Rexroth was soon dispatching reviews to the effect that the new writing was a flash in the literary pan. He attacked Kerouac in a *Time*'s piece, and in London, where the work of the beats was beginning to create a *sub rosa* stir, he gave notice, in an interview with the *Observer*, that Ginsberg had written himself out with *Howl*. Rexroth was known in those days both as the man-on-the-spot in San Francisco and as one of the first critics to survey the beat field; he supplied the data for most of the critics who surveyed it after him.

"It was really like a mess, trying to keep everything together," Ginsberg says. "First Rexroth and then Duncan, who was a little suspicious of us at the time because we were like invaders, who had made some sort of overrated local success, and he felt that the seriousness of the community already established in San Francisco wasn't being properly attended to. And it was a shame. Like in the sense that had there been a united front at that point —the older poets plus us from the East Coast—we would have been much more clear and impregnable in literary terms. And it would have helped in, like, high-teacup literary circles like *Encounter* and *Partisan Review*, where a good reception would have eased the whole intellectual torment. It would have made the younger professors of the fifties start reading real American poetry

and appreciating Williams then and there—and even start putting things together, like the end of McCarthyism with the beginning of a Whitmanic American spirit and a new consciousness.
But nobody but Eberhart picked up on it. All they saw was
a bunch of rebels who didn't know how to write, who didn't
have any tradition, who didn't have any real learning, going out
and bleeding and bleating their so-called free verse, which was
tried in 1910 and failed anyway, with Amy Lowell and whatnot.
The whole literary establishment just goofed. Completely. Like
they said that we all wrote the same. Denise Levertov was a
beatnik from San Francisco, which she resented. And then Robert
Duncan was a beatnik, and he resented *that* because he felt here
he'd been lumped with all these beatniks. It was terrible, all the
literary hangups that were going on."

Ginsberg left town in the middle of the argument. He and
Corso and Orlovsky had decided to drop in on Burroughs, who
was now living in Tangier, and, to earn the money to get them
there, Ginsberg shipped out again—this time to the Arctic Circle
as a yeoman storekeeper. Three months later, he was back in
San Francisco with fifteen hundred dollars in cash. The poets
took off in a matter of days, and they managed to cover Mexico,
Morocco, and most of Western Europe on Ginsberg's pay. When
they finally landed in New York, broke but worldly, Ginsberg
found a brand-new batch of *Howl* critics waiting for him. Louis
Simpson, who was poetry critic at the *Hudson Review*, as well
as the editor of Ginsberg's nightmares, had composed a *Howl*
parody—the hero as a battered, buttered pancake—as his review
of the collection, thereby inspiring a rash of inept parodies of
Ginsberg, Kerouac, and Corso, which were fast becoming textbook definitions of an apocryphal "beat style." Ginsberg's friend
John Hollander—they were students at Columbia together and
now Hollander was teaching there himself—had written in *his*
review that *Howl* was a "vulgar" poem of little artistic conse-
quence. And *Commentary* and *Partisan Review* had taken on the
beats with a conscientious vengeance that involved Norman

Podhoretz's confusing Norman Mailer's violent hipsterism with the beats' beatitude and laboring passionate comparisons of the aimless rebellions of the beatniks and the dedicated social revolutions of the thirties' intellectuals. Ginsberg says that a stereotype response to the new writing "spread from head to head like trench mouth." By the time he came home, it had already filtered down through the academic quarterlies and literary journals and was starting to make copy in the popular press.

Time, not unexpectedly, was the first of the news weeklies to pick up the trail of Ginsberg and his friends. The occasion was a visit that Ginsberg, Corso, and Orlovsky paid to Chicago in February of 1959, and *Time*'s account of it settled the question of beat poets for the commuters in much the same way that Diana Trilling's famous *Partisan Review* report of their sweat-shirt reading at Columbia, a few weeks later, settled the question of beat poetry for the literary powers. The three poets were in Chicago to read at a benefit for a magazine called *Big Table*, which had just been started, in the wake of a censorship scandal at the University of Chicago, by the editors of the school's censored quarterly review. *Time* dispensed with *Big Table* as a new beatnik publication and set its story at a ghastly cocktail party in the apartment of a Windy City financier with heavy aesthetic aspirations. Ginsberg, Corso, and Orlovsky were written into the festivities as a team of itinerant hucksters—Ginsberg was the "recognized leader of the pack of oddballs [*Time*, June 9] who celebrate booze, dope, sex, and despair, and who go by the name of beatniks"; Corso and Orlovsky followed him in as "two other shabbily dressed" members of the pack—and the next several paragraphs were devoted to snatches of mad conversation between the three beatniks and the financier's company. "It was all fried shoes. Like, it means nothing," the reporter concluded, quoting Corso. Predictably, most of the letters to the editor that promptly swamped *Time*'s mail room deplored this poetic state of affairs. (Ginsberg, Corso, and Orlovsky also wrote a long letter, which began, "You lie-creating Whore of Babylon!"; to *Parti-*

san Review, they simply sent the message, "The universe is a flower.") Unpredictably, *Time*'s piece, which was called "Manners and Morals," touched off a wave of fellow feeling in the underground. The repartee passed into beat folklore as a sort of poets' password, and today's hippies are still quoting it. Bob Dylan once told Ginsberg that the chorus of cocktail party introductions—"I'm Peter Orlovsky. I'm very fine and happy and crazy as a wild flower"; "I'm Allen Ginsberg, and I'm crazy like a daisy"; "I'm Gregory Corso, and I'm not crazy at all"—was the first indication for his generation of a "new consciousness" in America, and, in Dylan's case anyway, a better reason than most to begin reading poetry.

Ginsberg was considerably more volatile in those days before his pilgrimage East and his conversion to flower power and yogic temper control, and for a while he ran around New York arguing with his critics about the new writing. He was original, in any event, as a literary defender. He had a reputation for noise, he was notoriously long-winded and exhaustingly patient, and his critics, for the most part, tended to avoid him, slipping out of parties by the back door and crossing streets whenever they were fortunate enough to spot Ginsberg before he spotted them. Ginsberg eventually solved the problem by waging his wars by correspondence. His favorite letter—he saved copies of them all—was written to Hollander over the better part of a day in the fall of 1958:

> Dear John:
>
> Got your letter, slow answering since writing a little & invasion of people in apartment & too much mail, a lady in Michigan wanting to know if I believe in God, I have to answer everything, it's difficult. No, of course, communication's always there why not only a shit would be bugged, besides I've seen too much, I'm tired. It's just that I've tried to do too much explaining & get overwhelmed by the vastness of the

task, & sometimes what seems to be all the accumulated ill-will & evil vibrations in America (Kerouac got beaten up at the San Remo for his trouble in coming down there & making himself available). But to begin somewhere, I should might begin with one thing, simple (I hate to go back to it over & over, like revolving around my corpse, the construction of *Howl*). This may be corny to you, my concern with that, but I've got to begin somewhere & perhaps differences of opinion between us can be resolved by looking at that. See, for years before that, thinking in Williams line, which I found very helpful & quite real for what it is doing, the balance by ear of short lines formed of relatively natural ordinary notebook or conversation speech. "Xbalba" is fragments of mostly prose, written in a Mexican school copybook, over half a year—then rereading, picking out the purest thoughts, stringing them together, arranging them in lines suitably balanced—mostly measured by the phrase—that is, one phrase a line—you know it's hard to explain this because it's like painting and unless you do it like practicing a piano, you don't think in those terms & get the experience of trying to work that way, so you don't notice all the specific tricks—that anyone who works in that field gets to be familiar with—that's why I'm interested in Blackburn, Levertov, Creeley, Oppenheimer, all the *Black Mt.* people—they work steadily consistently trying to develop this line of goods, and each has a different interesting approach—they all stem out of Williams—but I can tell their lines apart they really are different—just as you can tell the difference between styles & approaches of abstract painters. When you tell me it's just a bore to you, that just cuts off communication, I mean I don't know what to say, I get embarrassed I feel you're being arbitrary & stubborn, it's some sort of ploy, & I just want to retreat & go about my work and stop explanations. Of course you may not be interested in this field of experiment, but that doesn't mean it's uninteresting to others, that it's categorically a bore. I ALSO believe it's the main "tradition," not that there is any tradition except what we make ourselves. But basically I'm not interested in tradition because I'm more interested in what I'm doing, what it's inevitable for me to do. This realization has given me perspective on what a vast sad camp the whole literary-critical approach of School has been—basically no one has insight into poetry techniques except people who are exercising them. But I'm straying at random. But I'm now getting bugged at people setting themselves up as scholars and authorities and *getting in the way* continues creative work or its understanding or circulation—there is not one article on the Beat or SF scene yet that has not been (pro and con) invalidated (including yours) by the basic fact that the author is just a big windbag not knowing what he's talking about—no technical background, no knowledge of the vast body of experimental work, published and unpublished (the unpublished is the best), no clear grasp of the various different schools of experiment all converging toward the same or similar end, all at once coming into intercommunication, no knowledge of the letters and conversations in between, not even the basic ability (like Podhoretz) to tell the difference between prosody and diction (as in his PR diatribes on spontaneous bop prosody confusing it with the use of hiptalk not realizing it refers to rhythmical construction of phrases or sentences). I mean where am I going to begin a serious explanation if I have to deal with such unmitigated stupid ignorant ill-willed inept vanity as that —someone like that wouldn't listen unless you hit him over the head with a totally new universe, but he's stuck in his own hideous world, I would try, but he scarcely has enough heart to hear—etc., etc.—so all these objections about juvenile delinquency, vulgarity, lack of basic education, bad taste, etc., etc., no form, etc., I mean it's impossible to discuss things like that —finally I get to see them as basically *wrong* (unscientific) so dependent on ridiculous provincial schoolboy ambitions & presuppositions and so lacking contact with practical fact—that it seems a sort of plot almost, a kind of organized mob stupidity —the final camp of its announcing itself as a representative of value or civilization or taste—I mean I give up, that's just too much fucking nasty brass. And you're guilty of that too, John, you've just got to drop it, and take me seriously, and listen to what I have to say. It doesn't mean you have to agree, or change your career or your writing, or anything hideous, it just means you've got to have the heart and decency to take people seriously and not depend *only* on your university experience for arbitrary standards of value to judge others by. It doesn't mean that you have to agree, that Free Verse is the Only Path of Prosodaic Experiment, or that Williams is a Saint, or I have some horrible magic secret (tho god knows I have, enough, this week with that damned buddist laughing gas, everybody has). Just enough to dig, you to dig, what others besides yourself are trying to do, and be interested in their work or not, but not to get in the way, in fact even encourage where you can see some value. And you're in a position to encourage, you teach, you shouldn't hand down limited ideas to younger minds—that was the whole horror of Columbia, there was just nobody there (maybe except Weaver) who had a serious involvement with advanced work in poetry. Just a bunch of Dilletantes. And THEY have the nerve to set themselves up as guardians of culture?!!? Why it's such a piece of effrontery —enough to make anyone Paranoiac, it's a mircle Jack or myself or anybody independent survived—tho god knows the toll in paranoia been high enough. All these grievances I'm pouring out to you. Well why revise.

Back to Howl: construction. After sick & tired of shortline free verse as not expressionistic enough, not swinging enough, can't develop a powerful enough rhythm. I simply turned aside, accidentally to writing part I of Howl, in solitude, diddling around with the form, thinking it couldn't be published anyway (queer content my parents shouldn't see, etc.) also it was out of my short-line line. But what I did taught my theory, I changed my mind about "measure" while writing it. Part one uses repeated base who, as a sort of kithera BLANG, homeric (in my imagination) to mark off each statement, with rhythmic unit. So that's experiment with longer & shorter variations on a fixed base—the principle being, that each line has to be contained within the elastic of one breath—with suitable punctuatory expressions where the rhythm has built up enough so that I have to let off steam by building a longer climactic line in which there is a jazzy ride. All the ear I've ever developed goes into the balancing of those lines. The interesting moments when the rhythm is sufficiently powerful pushing ahead so I can ride out free and drop the key that holds it together. The method of keeping a long line still all poetic and not prosey is the concentration and compression of basically imageistic notations into surrealist or cubist phrasing, like hydrogen jukeboxes. Ideally anyway. Good example of this is Gregory's great (I swear) Coit Tower ode. Lines have greater poetic density. But I've tried to keep the language sufficiently dense in one way or another—use of primitive naive grammer (expelled for

crazy), elimination of prosey articles & syntactical sawdust, juxta-
position of cubist style images, or hot rhythm. Well then
Part II. Here the basic repeated word is Moloch. The long line
is now broken up into component short phrases with ! rhythmical punctuation. The key repeat BLANG word is repeated
internally in the line (basic rhythm sometimes emerging
/—/—) but the rhythm depends mostly on the internal Moloch
repeat. Lines here lengthened—a sort of free verse prose poetry
STANZA form invented or used here. This builds up to climax
(Visions! Omens! etc.) and then falls off in coda, Part III,
perhaps an original invention (I thought so then but this type
of thinking is vain & shallow anyway) to handling of long line
(for the whole poem is an experiment in what you can do with
the long line—the whole book is)—: : : that is, a phrase base
rhythm (I'm with you etc.), followed as in litany by a response
of the same length (Where you're madder etc.), then repeat
of base over and over with the response elongating itself slowly,
still contained within the elastic of one breath till the stanza
(for it is a stanza form there, I've used variations of it since)
building up like a pyramid, an emotion crying siren sound,
very appropriate to the expressive appeal emotion I felt (a
good healthy emotion said my analyst at that time, to dis-
pose once and for all of that idiotic objection)—anyway, building up to the climax where there's a long long long line,
pentultimate, too long for one breath, where I open out and
give the answer (O starry spangled shock of Mercy the eternal
war is here. All this rather like a jazz mass, I mean the con-
ception of rhythm not derived from jazz directly, but if you
listen to jazz you get the idea (in fact specifically old trum-
pet solo on a JATP Can't Get Started side)—well all this is
built like a brick shithouse and anybody can't hear the mystic
id as I told you—guess I meekly inferred Trilling, who is absolutely lost in poetry, is got a tin ear, and that's so obviously
true, I get sick and tired I read 50 reviews of Howl and not
one of them written by anyone with enough technical interests
to notice the fucking obvious construction of the poem, all
the details besides (to say nothing of the various esoteric
classical allusions built in like references to Cezanne's theory
of composition, etc., etc.)—that I GIVE UP and anybody
henceforth comes up to me with a silly look in his eye and
begins bullshitting about morals and sociology & tradition

and technique & JD—I mean I je ne sais plus parler—the horrible irony of all these jerks who can't *read* trying to lecture me (us) on FORM)

Kerouac has his own specific method of construction of prose which he has persued for a decade now and I have yet to see one piece of criticism taking that into account, or even interested enough to realize he has one & its implications in how it relates to the rhythm of his prose—much less how his method alters and develops chronologically from book to book, what phases it goes thru, which changes one would en- counter in so prolonged a devoted experiment as his (rather like Gertrude Stein)—but nobody's interested in literature, in technique, all they think about is their goddamn lousy ideas of what they preconceive writing to be about and IM SICK OF LISTENING TO THAT AND READING ABOUT THAT AND UNLESS THERE IS MORE COOPERATION FROM THE SUPPOSEDLY RESPONSIBLE PARTIES IN UNIVERSITIES & MAGAZINES I ABSOLUTELY CUT OUT AND REFUSE TO MY HEART WRUNG POEMS TO THE DIRTY HANDS AND MINDS OF THESE BASTARDS AND THEY CAN TAKE THEIR FUCKING literary tradition AND SHOVE IT UP THEIR ASS—I don't need them and they don't need me and I'm sick of putting myself out and being put down and hit on the head by jerks who have no interest but their ridiculous devilish social careers and MONEY MONEY MONEY which is the root of the EVIL here in America and I'M MAD.

Footnote to Howl is too lovely & serious a joke to try to explain. The built in rhythmic exercise should be clear, it's basically a repeat of the Moloch section. It's dedicated to my mother who died in the madhouse and it says I loved her anyway & that even in worst conditions life is holy. The exaggerations of the statements are appropriate, and anybody who doesn't understand the specific exaggerations will never understand "Rejoice in the Lamb" or Lorca's "Ode to Whit- man" or Mayakovsky's "At the Top of My Voice" or Artaud's "Pour En Finir Avec le Jugement de Dieu" or Apollinaire's "inspired bullshit" or Whitman's madder passages or anything, anything, anything about international modern spirit in poesy to say nothing about the international tradition in prosody

which has grown up nor the tradition of open prophetic
bardic poetry which 50 years has sung like an angel over the
poor soul of the world while all sorts of snippy cats castrates
pursue their good manners and sell out their own souls and
the spirit of god who now DEMANDS sincerity and hell fire
take him who denies the voice in his soul—except that it's
all a kindly joke & the universe disappears after you die so
nobody gets hurt no matter how little they allow themselves
to live and blow on this Earth.

Anyone noticing the construction & series of poems in Howl
would then notice that the next task I set myself to was adapt-
ing that kind of open long line to tender lyric feelings and
short form, so next is Supermarket in Calif. where I pay hom-
age to Whitman in realistic terms (eyeing the grocery boys)
and it's a little lyric, and since it's almost prose it's cast in
form of prose paragraphs like St. Perse—and has nobody
noticed that I was aware enough of that to make that shift
there. Nor that I went on in the next poem Transcription of
Organ music to deliberately write a combo of prose and poetry
some lines indented which are poetic and some lines not but
paragraphed like prose to see what could be done with Absolute transcription of spontaneous material, transcription of
sensual data (organ) at a moment of near Ecstasy, not, nor
has anyone noticed that I have technically developed my
method of transcription (as Cezanne developed sketching) so
that I could transcribe at such moments & try to bring back
to the poor suffering world what rare moments exist, and that
technical practice has led to a necessary spontaneous method
of transcription which will pass in and out of poetry and so
needs a flexible form—its own natural form unchanged—to
preserve the moment alive and uncensured by the arbitrary
ravenings of conceptual or preconceptual or post-censuring-out-
of-embarrassment so called intelligence? Anyway there is a
definite experiment in FORM FORM FORM and not a
ridiculous idea of what form *should* be like. And it is an example that has all sorts of literary precedents in French poetry,
in Hart Crane, in—but this whole camp of FORM is so ridiculous that I am ashamed to have to use the word to justify
what is THERE. (and only use it in a limited academic context but would not dream of using this kindergarten terminol-

ogy in poets from whom I *learn*—Kerouac, Burroughs or Corso —who start to new worlds of their own invention with minds so Columbian & holy that I am ashamed of my own academic Tribe that is so superciliously hung on COLLEGE that it has lost touch with living creation.)

The next problem attacked in the book is to build up a rhythmical drive in long lines without dependence on repetition of any words and phrases, who's, Moloch's, or Holy's, a drive forward to a climax and conclusion and to do it spontaneously (well, I've broken my typewriter on this explanation I continue on Peter's—a twenty minute task ("Sunflower") with 15 years practice behind—to ride out on the breath ryhthm without any artificial built in guides or poles or diving boards or repetition except the actual rhythm, and to do it so that both long long lines, and lone lines, and shorter 10 word lines all have the same roughly weight, and balance each other out, and anybody take the trouble to read Sutra out will see it does that & the Come of the rhythmic buildup is "You were never no locomotive Sunflower, you were a sunflower, and you locomotive (pun) you were a locomotive, etc.," And furthermore at this point in the book I am sick of preconceived literature and only interested in *writing* the actual process and technique, wherever it leads, and the various possible experiments in composition that are in my path—and if anybody still is confused in what literature is let it be hereby announced once for all in the 7 Kingdoms that that's what it is—Poetry is what poets write, and not what other people think they should write.

The next poem America takes off on the free line and is an attempt to make combinations of short and long lines, very long lines and very short lines, something I've always wanted to do but previously had to depend on sustained rhythmical buildup to carry the structure of the poem forward. But In America I rely on discrete separate statements, rather than one long madbreath forward. Here as always however the measure, the meter, of each line, the think the thing that makes it a complete line, and the thing that balances each line with its neighbors is that each (with tactical exceptions) is ONE SPEECH BREATH—an absolute physical measure as absolute as the ridiculous limited little accent or piddling syllable count. And in this I've gone forward from Williams because I literally measure each line by the physical breath—each one breath statement, dictated by what has to be said, in relation and balance to the previous rhythmic statement.

The next task the book includes is the Greyhound poem which is an attempt to apply the method with all tricks, long with short lines mixed, some repetition some not, some lyric, some Bardic, some surrealist or cubist phrasing, some pure imagistic-Williams notation—all apply all this to a realistic solid work proletarian common experience situation & come up with a classical elegiac poem in modern rhythm & tricks etc. Also to make a nonhowling poem with separate parts etc.

So all this ends up to a handbook on various experiments with the possibilities of an expressive long line, and perhaps carries on from where Whitman in US left off with his long lines. At least I've in part III Howl attempted one visible organic stanza construction. Pound complains that Whitman was not interested enough in developing his line, I have tried to rescue long line for further use—tho at the moment (since last year I've abandoned it for a totally different mode than I've ever used, a totally wild page of free verse dictated by the immediate demands of spontaneous notation, with its appearance or form on the page determined by the structure of thought, rather than the aural quality primarily.

Latter's unclear I'll start over. The poetry in Williams has depended a lot on little breath groups for its typographical organization, and in Howl an extension into longer breaths (which are more natural to me than William's short simple talks)—there is another possible approach to the measure of the line—which is, not the way you would *say* it, a thought, but the way you would think it—i.e., we think rapidly, in visual images as well as words, and if each successive thought were transcribed in its confusion (really its ramification) you get a slightly different prosody than if you were talking slowly.

This still not clear—if you talk fast and excitedly you get weird syntax & rhythms, just like you think, or nearer to what you think. Not that everybody's think process is consciously the same—everybody's got a different consciousness factory—but the attempt here is to let us see—to transcribe the thought all at once so that its ramifications appear on the page much as into a paradigm in grammar books—example, from last

poem (Laughing gas—an attempt to transcribe that experience
of the dis-appearance of chilicosm when consciousness is
anesthetized, as an instance of what maybe happens at death)

> The Bloomfield police car
> > with its idiot red light
> > revolving on its head
> > balefully at eternity—
> > > gone in an instant
> > > —simultaneous
> > > appearance of bankrobbers
> > at the Twentieth Century Bank
> The fire engines screaming
> > toward an old lady's
> > burned-in-her-bedroom
> > today apocalypse
> > > tomorrow
> > mickey mouse cartoons—
>
> I'm disgusted! It's unbelievable!
> How could it all be so
> > horrible & funny?
> > > It's a dirty joke!
> The whole universe is a shaggy dog story
> > with a weird ending that
> > begins   again
> > > till you get the point
> "IT was a dark and gloomynight"
> > "in every direction in and
> > > out"
> > > > "You take the high road
> > and I'll take the low"
> > > everybody in the same
> fantastic Scotland of the mind—
> > consciousness
>
> Gary Snyder, Jack, thou Zens
> > split opn existence
> > and laugh and cry—
> what's shock? what's measure?
> > when the mind's irrational

—follow the blinking lights
   of contrariety—
              etc., etc.

Well I haven't done enough work yet in this direction, I want
to get a wild page, as wild and as clear (really clear) as the
mind—no forcing the thoughts into straightjacket—sort of a
search for the rhythm of the thoughts & their natural occur-
rence & spacings & notational paradigms. Naturally when you
read it aloud it also turns out to have intricate aural rhythm.
But this is just an experiment—and naturally, this type writing
gives thought an artificial form—the mere crystallizing it on
page does—but to attempt to reproduce the droppings of the
mind on the page—to work freely with this kind of direction—
you see—you see—it's fascinating to me.

*   *   *

Well what's all this leading up to? I don't know yet I'm
just obviously blowing off steam. Yes, back to Xbalba. If you,
one, is interested in certain awkward natural style, for reasons,
then the fact the Xbalba is "carefully made" is its minor
virtue—it's technically no improvement on Williams, except
it's application of free verse to wordsworthian meditation long-
poem—tintern abbey type, or byronic meditation on ruins.
But the real technical advance is in the long line poems, they
proceed inevitably and naturally from the earlier poems, it's
just a sort of COMPOUND imagism—compounded cubist
images, and compounded rhythmic long lines. By hindsight. If
I ever worried about technique in advance I wouldn't be able
to write a line—THAT kind of worry. My worries are more
practical having to do with the problem of breath and notation
and the freeing of myself from preconceptions as to literary
Style. The beauty of the writing is as Williams says, the invention, the discovery of new appropriate forms, the discovery
of something you DON'T know, rather than the synthesis repetition of the things you do already know. It's a jump up forward
into life, unknown future life, not—not an old spinster hung up
on her one virgin experience and endlessly crooning it to herself (while the robber unknown's waiting under the bed.) Any
poem I write that I have written before, in which I don't
discover something new (psychically) and maybe formally, is
a waste of time, it's not living. I mean to get to the point of

finally being frank and including queer material in the poems with a liberation, socially and psychically etc.—of expanding the ares of reality I can deal with in the poems rather than shrinking back—(one reason I dig Gregory—he'll write about *anything*, socks, army, food, Arnold, Loony—so he also now writes to the ONE GREAT POEM about the Bomb. He's extended the area of poetic experience further out than anyone I know—my own area is still rather limited to literary aesthetic hangovers from stupid education experiences. At least he writes, (as Koch coincidentally demanded in poem Fresh Air) a poem about PANTS. Williams precise real images are such a relief after affected iambics, but PANTS is such a relief after hard real Williams—a new Romanticism in bud. But expanding the area you can deal with directly, especially to include all the irrational of subjective mystic experience & queerness & pants—in other words individuality—means again (as it did for Whitman) the possibility in a totally brainwashed age where all communication is subject to mass control (including especially including off-beat type talks in universities & places like Partisan)—means again at last the possibility of Prophetic poetry—it's no miracle—all you have to know is what you actually think & feel & every sentence will be a revelation—everybody else is so afraid to talk even if they have any feelings left. & this kind of Bardic frankness prophecy is what Whitman called for in American poets—them to take over from Priests—lest materialism & mass-production of emotion drown america (which it has) & we become what he called the Fabled Damned among nations which we have—and it's been the cowardice and treason & abandonment of the poetic natural democratic soul by the poets themselves that's caused the downfall & doom of the rest of the world too—an awful responsibility. It's not that Podhoritz & the rest of the whores are just a passing phenomenon of vulgarity like transient editorials in the daily news, it's the very Poison that'll permanently sicken the mental soul here & has sickened the nation beyond recovery already—simply nobody taking responsibility for their own real thought—nothing but a lot of trillinguesque evasions with communist doubletalk about moral imagination, a cheap trick to suppress their own inside irrational Life & Poetry & reduce everything to the intellectual standard of a Time magazine report on the present happiness and proper role of the American Egghead who's getting paid now & has a nice job & fits in with the whole silly system—well it's no loss to have it already blown out from under them by the ridiculous collapse of the American Century after Sputnik— I suppose there's a new "examination of conscience" going on somewhere in their heads & they'll come up with a worried bald set of polemics while gay prophet Corso starves ignored in Paris. AND I'M not OVERSTATING CORSO's magical importance. So anyway there is this Grove anthology of all these poets (about 30) coming out in a year and if you call that a BORE again I swear I'll write you a letter goofier than this & twice as exasperated—unless you really *believe* that— in which case I give up but god knows I havent tried—and while I'm on the subject, I'm sick of reading articles on Beat or SF poetry accusing me or anyone of inability to express my self, incoherence or jimmydeanesque oral blocking, inability to communicate, etc.—I certainly refuse to get any more involved with the stupidity of other people in petty mad literary arguments and so for that reason have refrained (tho god knows I get messianic critical article inpulses) from writing insane long articles refuting this and that misunderstanding, etc etc. better save my energy for god knows what, at least something real, a letter, or a poem agh, I wind up fuming in solitary. Well I know I'm raving, but I've saved it all up for you. And is Trilling behind all this mass stupidity about poetry, at least in NY?

*   *   *

All these people [Kerouac, Corso, Olson, Creeley, Snyder, Whalen, Levertov, Zukofsky, Blackburn, Burroughs, McClure, Wieners, Duncan, and other writers whose work Ginsberg discussed in a long section of the letter not included here] should have long ago been having books out in NY & reviewed seriously everywhere & the lack of their material has left the atmosphere poisoned by bad poetry and bad people and bad criticism—and the criticism! incredible after 2 decades of new criticism & the complete incompetence to evaluate & recognise anything new—nothing but lame sociological bullshit in response to Jack's prose or my poetry—or total amnesia with Gregory's or Creeley's & Olson's etc. All the universities been fucking dead horse for decades and this is *Culture*!? Yet prosidy & conceptions of poetry been chang-

ing for half a century already and what a columbia instructor
can recognise in Pound he can't see in Olson's method, what
he can see in Lorca or Apollinaire he can't see in Howl—it's
fantastic. You call this education? I call it absolute brainwashed
bullshit. Not saying that either Olson or Howl are Lorca or
Pound—I'm saying there's a recognizable continuity of method
—yet I have to listen to people giving me doublethink gobble-
dygook about why don't I write poems with form, construction,
something charming and carefully made. O Lawrence thou
should be living at this hour! and diana trilling in public correspondence with that eminent representative of the younger
generation Podhoritz about Lawrence! It's a vast Trap. and
god save the poor young students who know nothing but that
mad incestuous atmosphere. I could go on all night. What
else what else? I don't have your review here or I'd try to work
in and out of that. and some jerk named Brustein who
TEACHES at columbia writing in a new money money money
magazine Horizon attacking the Cult of Unthink, grandscale
vicious attack on Stanislavsky Method, abstract painting (bed-
fellows!) & beat writing drooling on about how I express every
degradation but the one humane one Loneliness—I mean some
completely inaccurate irrelevant piece of journalism!—ignor-
ing big queer lonely lyrics about Whitman & Moloch in whom
I sit lonely cocksucking—just goes on and says this here vicious
incoherent Ginsberg refuses to admit he's lonely. He
TEACHES! is such a shit allowed on this earth? The whore
of Babylon's befallen us! Run for your life! and in Highclass
Partisan, Podhoretz (I keep coming back to him it seems he
has collected all the garbage in one mind, archetype) quoting
me about Jack's "spontaneous bop prosody" proceeds to attack
it instead of trying to figure what i mean—because I put it
there as a tip, a helpful hint to criticism, a kindly extraverted
gesture—and winds up all balled up confusing jack's *diction*
& use of the mind's hiptalk to itself with the *rhythm* of the
consequent sentences—This sort of ignorant Babel in partisan
Review—and they tell me he'll be editor someday? Could that
be true? Well they deserve it if they put up with that Yahoo
type creepy mentality. I'm sick of the creeps bugging the scene,
my scene, America's scene, we only live once, why put up with
that grubby type ambitious vanity. Ugh. It's too ignoble. Take

it away. I'll take a sick junky any day to this hoarde of half educated deathly academicians. Not *one* yet, not ONE in all the colleges, magazines, book pages has said anything real, has got the point, either of spirit or prosody (what a camp word— I'm sorry I keep using it—it really is that—but *another* way) NOT ONE. And this is the product of the schools of the richest nation of the earth, this is the Intelligentsia that's supposed to run the world, inc. moon? It's a monster shambles.

Complaints, complaints, you hear them on a summers day. Pound is absolutely right . . . With Usra. The whole problem is these types want money & security and not ART.

Well I don't know where to go from here, I've unloaded it all on your head . . . tho you asked for it . . . on the other hand that's what we're here for, why not have a ball.

I did all this so I wouldn't be involved in endless statement when we met, explanations, better shit it all out at once.

*   *   *

yours in the kingdom of music
Nella Grebsnig
the birds have eaten the berries

Max's Kansas City, on the corner of Eighteenth Street and Park Avenue South, opened in 1966 for the purpose of serving steak and ambiance to the amalgam of artists, writers, film makers, underground eccentrics, pop intelligentsia and rich, beautiful people who then comprised the New York avant-garde. The house specials were a big slab of rump steak—with baked potato, chick peas, and all the salad you could eat—for two dollars and fifty cents, free leftover Napoleons at four in the morning, and a bulky collection of junk sculpture and assemblages on loan from the clientele, and Max's instantly became a hangout because of them. Like "21," it was soon divided up, with mysterious logic, by the cognescenti into areas of varying status and desirability. A second-story dining room was left for tourists and uptown patrons of no special significance, who were hustled up the stairs and out of sight before they could intrude on the atmosphere, while downstairs, peripheral members of the scene were consigned to a long bar in a black, narrow passageway. It was in the back room of Max's, lit death-red by one of Flaven's neon constructions, that the celebrities of the avant-garde held court. (It was also in the back room that Maretta occasionally would abandon her Buddhist vows with a sirloin steak.)

Max's was crowded with its late-night regulars when Ginsberg dropped by, a little after one, on his way home from Basil Bunting's hotel. A young man in blue jeans, stationed behind a John Chamberlain made out of mangled car fenders, was screening strangers, and he waved Ginsberg on as he stepped out of the gloom to examine two nervous-looking couples with *Cactus Flower* playbills in their hands. Ginsberg, who was still trailing his Harvard scarf, edged his way along the bar, stopping every few feet to chat with people from the neighborhood. With the advent of the love people, the tinkle of bells and the smell of flowers had been grafted onto the pop ambiance of the Kansas City, and tonight two girls, who were leaning decoratively against the wall in their kirtan clothes, sang out a Sanskrit hello as Ginsberg passed, and a man from a journal of psychedelic exploration called *Inner Space* filled him in on the issue that was about to hit the downtown stands.

Ginsberg's friends from the Bunting reading already were in the back room, waiting for him. Robert Creeley and his wife had driven down earlier with Corso and Bunting's English publisher, and they were huddled around a couple of pulled-together tables, deep in a mutually wary conversation with some late arrivals from Andy Warhol's studio. A Warhol movie star, who called himself René Ricard, was chattering to Mrs. Creeley about the *petits ennuis* of fame, and Ginsberg's erstwhile boarder, Beelzebub, was holding forth on the function of the diabolic in an Aquarian age. Across the room, bathed in neon, Warhol and one of his young disciples were sitting in a booth, listening to a skinny, frenetic blonde in octagonal sunglasses. The blonde, under the name Tiger Morse, had recently made a fortune designing hula skirts of aluminum shavings and signed sets of electrified breastplates. At the moment, she was trying to encourage some public sentiment on behalf of a little Russian trawler which had been seized in Alaskan territorial waters and was in serious danger of having to relinquish its tuna-fish catch to the American authorities. She had just given up on a middle-aged couple in the next booth (the couple had slipped into the back room by mistake and were now gulping down their coffee and signaling desperately for a waitress to retrieve them), and she was in the middle of apprising Warhol of the situation when Ginsberg, who had spotted the artist through a haze of reddish smoke, ambled over with a cup of tea and slid into the booth beside him.

"*Hare Krishna*," Ginsberg said, giving Warhol a slap on the back.

Warhol winced slightly, and he continued staring at Miss Morse as she flapped her arms in imitation of a tuna death throe. At the end of her story, Warhol uttered a low, carefully modulated "wow." The word was ambiguous as to its moral stance.

Miss Morse flapped on to another booth.

"Well, that's the fishing business," Ginsberg said.

Warhol nodded, moving his head to the right by about a quarter of an inch. A lock of his hair, which was dyed a dry, silvery white, drooped slowly down onto his forehead, and his eyes, which, like Miss Morse's eyes, were very nearly hidden by a pair of dark sunglasses, blinked once. He was wearing a thin striped T-shirt, dungarees, black motorcycle boots, and a look of relentless passivity. A layer of thick, chalky make-up on Warhol's nose was beginning to melt.

"Well, you're looking the same," Ginsberg said cheerfully.

Warhol nodded again.

"Actually, I think Andy's looking a little tired," Warhol's companion, whose name was Henry, said. Henry himself was dressed up in his great-grandfather's Spanish-American War uniform, and he was munching happily on a hamburger. He told Ginsberg that, having at last escaped the confines of a Swiss finishing school, where the bedtime snack was likely to consist of *pâté en croûte*, he was devoting all of his energy to "making the scene" in New York.

"You should have been with us tonight," Henry said. "We were at Andy's new discotheque. It was wild."

"I was at a poetry reading at the Guggenheim." Ginsberg grinned. "You should have been *there*."

"Wow," Warhol said. He seemed on the point of elaborating, but just then Corso, who had previously been occupied with a buxom, back-room hippie maiden, came reeling toward him, waving around a double Scotch.

"I know you," Corso said, snarling.

Ginsberg edged over on the bench and patted a place for him.

Corso sat down, furious. "I know you, mister, and I don't like you," he said.

"Hey, that's not a very friendly thing to say to Andy," Ginsberg said. He looked from Corso to Warhol, who was, to all intents, expressionless, and back to Corso. "You mad at Andy or something?"

Corso ignored him. "I know all about you pop people," he said. "How you use people. How you make them superstars of New York and then you drop them. You're evil." Corso emptied his glass, called to a waitress (who was hovering by the booth, listening) for a refill, and began again. "You're making a social scene and Ginsberg here—he's making a freak scene." He wagged a finger at Warhol. "You and all those rich women and faggots and Velvet Undergrounds, and Allen with Swamis and Fugs— you've all lost me."

Ginsberg put his arm around Corso and began chanting something soothing.

Corso hung his head. "Let me tell you about Allen," he said to Henry, who dropped his hamburger. "Allen is my best friend, and I don't even like *him* any more." Then he poked Ginsberg.

"You know why, Allen?"—Ginsberg shook his head—"Because you sing bad. You're always singing. Maretta sings good, Allen, but you don't sing good."

Ginsberg looked down and said "*Om.*"

"And you know what else?" Corso said, leaning past Ginsberg and glaring into Warhol's sunglasses. "You never give anything away. The Diggers—you know the Diggers?—they give *everything* away. They're all right. They share. What have *you* ever given away?"

"So you *are* mad at Andy," Ginsberg said. "Come on, Gregory, what are you mad at Andy for?"

Corso shrugged.

Ginsberg turned to Warhol. "Do you feel that's true? That you're evil? That you never give anything away?"

Warhol didn't answer.

"Andy means no," Ginsberg said.

Corso jumped up. "Hey, where's my girl? I've lost my girl!" he shouted.

"Take it easy." Ginsberg pointed to the Creeleys' table. "She's right there. She's not going anyplace."

"Watch me get her, Mr. Warhol," Corso called over his shoulder as he headed for the girl, who was nibbling on some chick peas, and began tugging at her sleeve. He was back in a minute. The girl smiled absently while Corso installed her on his lap.

"How do you like that?" Corso demanded. "Two minutes to get a girl. I bet you never got a girl in two minutes." He thought for a moment and added, "This is—let's see now—"

"Cynthia," the girl said.

Corso reached over and tapped Warhol on the arm. "What's your name? I want to introduce you to Cynthia," he said.

"His name is Andy—Andy Warhol," Ginsberg said.

"Mr. Warhol, this is Cynthia, my girl friend," Corso said.

Warhol was staring into space.

"Aha," Corso screamed. "So you won't look at Cynthia. You're *scared* of me."

Ginsberg explained that Warhol was a man of little or no kinetic inclination.

"No, he's scared of me," Corso said. "Everybody's scared of me. What's wrong with everybody? People didn't use to be so scared. People used to look like gods. People used to run around smoking and drinking firewater. Everybody had fire coming out of their noses. And now look at everybody. They're scared of me. Even my oldest friend—*you're* scared of me. It's because you know I'm right."

Ginsberg put his hand on the back of Corso's neck and began massaging it. Cynthia looked longingly in the direction of her chick peas.

In a minute Corso said, "Do you know why I'm right, Mr. Warhol? Do you know why I'm hard on you? It's because I've found the missing link. Do you know what that is? Seeds! I went all the way back from the Egyptians to the Sumerians to the neoliths—all the way back to the apes. And then I discovered seeds. Morning-glory seeds. The last ape got stoned on morning-glory seeds and became human. It was only when seeds came. I bet you didn't know that."

"Tell me, Gregory, why are you so angry at Andy?" Ginsberg said. He was still rubbing Corso's neck.

Cynthia started to squirm.

"You know what's wrong with you?" Corso said, stroking Cynthia with one hand and shaking the other at Warhol. "Too many lonely women are in love with you. You use them. You give them dope and then you leave them. You don't *love* them."

"Oh, come on," Ginsberg interrupted. "*I've* been here— you haven't. You don't really know what's happened here. He doesn't *give* people dope. He's tolerant of people *on* dope. You're not being fair. And anyway, he *gives* money away."

"Come on, Cynthia," Corso said. He slid the girl off his lap and grabbed her hand. Then he glared at Ginsberg. "You're my best friend, but I don't want to talk to you any more tonight.

I want to talk to *Cynthia*. I'm going to tell her how pretty she is"—he grinned, toothlessly, at Cynthia, who blushed—"and beg her to come home with me. Hey, Allen, is it all right if Cynthia comes home tonight?"

"It would be groovy," Ginsberg said.

"And I don't want to talk to you either," Corso told Warhol. "I'm glad I'm not in your faggoty scene. It's all show. I see that beautiful blond angelic face of yours and it's got a snarl on it. It's an ugly face."

Corso and Cynthia disappeared.

Ginsberg looked at Warhol for a minute, and then patted the painter's limp hand. "He's probably right, but he's drunk," Ginsberg said.

Warhol was speechless.

"Did he hurt your feelings?" Ginsberg said. "He didn't *really* hurt your feelings, did he?"

Warhol was still staring into the smoke, but a trace of a sad expression had settled on his face.

Ginsberg burst out laughing. "He *did* hurt your feelings," Ginsberg shouted, flinging his arms around Warhol and enveloping him in a long, happy hug. "You've got *feelings*! What do you know—feelings!" Then he said, "There's a really groovy poet in town who I think you should meet."

Chapter 4

In 1960, when Ginsberg came home from a tour of South America which had begun as a short, free trip to a writers' conference in Santiago and had lasted half a year, he found that he and Orlovsky were invited to Boston to address the annual convention of something called the Group for the Advancement of Psychiatry. The psychiatrists in GAP, as they referred to themselves, had already exhausted such subjects as "criminality among Negroes" and "adjustment problems of Puerto Ricans" at their earlier symposiums, and consequently they had voted to devote themselves *this* year to the beat generation—and, according to their invitation, to the psychic peculiarities of Ginsberg and Orlovsky in particular. Ginsberg was delighted. In South America, he had kept a journal of his feelings and fantasies under ayahuasca, and he had just been editing his poems "Laughing Gas," "Mescaline," and "Lysergic Acid" for his new collection, *Kaddish and Other Poems*.

He was extremely curious to hear what the psychiatrists would have to say about them.

The night he arrived in Boston, Ginsberg gave a long reading from most of the texts and poems that he had ever written under, after, and about drugs. Some of the younger doctors at the meeting, fresh from medical-school courses in abnormal personality, concluded that Ginsberg was textbook crazy and dismissed him as a case of no special significance, but the older psychiatrists— "out of a Viennese tradition of enormous culture, like where Freud wrote books on Leonardo and Dostoevski, and everybody sat around listening to Mozart and Beethoven all the time, and psychiatry and the discovery of the unconscious was like a profound humanist revolution," Ginsberg says—were apparently intrigued by him. They told Ginsberg that what he had accomplished through drugs was, in their terms, a complete disintegration of the ego structure, a descent into the id, and then a re-creation and integration of the ego structure, slightly changed. Sir Humphrey Osmond, from Saskatchewan, was particularly interested in Ginsberg's drug experiments. Osmond was the doctor who had taken peyote with Chief Frank Takes Gun, of the Native American Church, and had, in turn, given the hallucinogen to Aldous Huxley in the experiments on which Huxley later based his book *The Doors of Perception*. At the moment, Osmond was conducting pioneer LSD research with his patients at the Saskatchewan Hospital. Both he and a New York analyst by the name of Edward Hornick—Hornick knew Ginsberg well, and had been responsible, in part, for his invitation to Boston —suggested that Ginsberg might want to meet a psychologist who was teaching at Harvard's Center for the Study of Human Behavior and experimenting there, on a grant from Sandoz Pharmaceuticals, with mushrooms containing psilocybin. Ginsberg already had taken LSD (which is a chemical synthesis of the mushroom) in 1959, at the invitation of a Stanford research psychologist who was recording its effects on creativity, but he had never tried the mushroom itself. (Psilocybin mushrooms

were reputedly "not very tasty," he says.) As soon as he was
back in New York, he wrote to the psychologist, saying that he
would be honored to participate in an experiment.

One week later, Timothy Leary knocked at Ginsberg's door.

"I was absolutely delighted that a big professor of psychology,
or whatever he was, would deign to come down to the Lower
East Side," Ginsberg says now. "He said that he was interested
in *my* experience with drugs, and he was like seriously concerned about how to handle this new LSD thing, concerned that
it be done with sincerity and openness rather than as some sort
of manipulative scientific game. He was a little naïve though—
like he had no idea that every poet in San Francisco had lived
with Indians and taken peyote and mescaline long ago. Or that
everybody was smoking pot. *He'd* never smoked pot. It was astonishing. He knew nothing about it, or junk, or the whole
underground. So I gave him some pot and we sat down and had
this long scholarly talk. I was surprised that he was such a jivey,
friendly, amiable, open guy. And I saw right away that he saw me
as like a wise Jewish patriarch type with a family, rather than a
creepy beatnik. So I decided to go to Boston and experiment
with him . . . I had been so conditioned to the underground
beatnik drug scene that the scene at Harvard was very strange.
Leary had this big, beautiful house, and everybody there was
wandering around like it was some happy cocktail party, which
was a little shocking to me at first because I still thought of
myself as like a big, serious religious meditator. And then they
were all so cheerful and optimistic and convinced that their kind
of experiment would be welcomed as a polite, scholarly, socially
acceptable, perfectly reasonable pursuit and would spread through
the university and be automatically taken on as part of the
curriculum. Like Leary couldn't conceive of meeting any academic opposition. I kept saying, 'You have no idea what you're
going to meet, what you're up against,' but he was already think-

ing in terms of, 'We'll turn on Schlesinger and then we'll turn on Kennedy'—in terms like that. So I wanted to calm him down a little, and I said, 'Why not begin by turning artists on?' People who could articulate their experiences and manifest them in some way or other, people like Robert Lowell, or Dizzy Gillespie, or Thelonious Monk, or Kerouac, or Burroughs. And so one week he came down to New York with some acid, and we made a big list and went around turning people on. Lowell we gave only a small dose to, and he had a very nice message—he said '*Amor vincit omnia.*' Gillespie thought it was so groovy that he brought his whole band to turn on. When I asked him, 'How'd you like it?' he said, 'Anything that gets you high, man, is great!' But Monk—the next time I saw *him* he said, 'Man, you better give me something stronger than that next time, because I didn't feel nothing, nothing at all.' "

Late in 1961, with *Naked Lunch* in the bookstores, and LSD in the Harvard Yard, one of Ginsberg's friends from *Big Table* announced—"pretty truly," Ginsberg says—that the beat revolution was over. Ginsberg headed for India. He was gone, off and on, for the next four years.

Chapter 5

The first Greater New York Be-In and Easter of 1967 fell on the same day. It was a warm and sunny Sunday. The snow that had been falling all week had vanished overnight, and the sharp March winds had finally blown themselves to sea, leaving the city fresh and the sky clear. Nobody seemed to mind the mud, which was ankle-deep in parts of Central Park. There were rumors, in fact, among the *emigré* love missionaries who had hitchhiked east from the Haight-Ashbury, that Michael Bowen's guru had made a good deal with the weather gods again. Only ten weeks had passed since their own Gathering of the Tribes in San Francisco, but the word had spread and Easter never really stood a chance against it. While the rest of the city trudged up and down Fifth Avenue, some thirty thousand New York beings came to the old Sheep Meadow in the park to celebrate—and most of them came painted and glittering, trailing daffodils and wreathed in incense smoke. They were in full frolic when Ginsberg arrived at the Be-In early in the afternoon. Boys and girls with horns and drums and bells were making music all over the meadow. (It had been decided, after ten weeks of reflection and steamy theorizing by a crop of junior ontologists, that at a truly *human* Be-In everybody would be free to do his own thing—to wit, there was no bandstand in the park today.) Middle-aged strangers were dancing with each other, gleefully erotic. Here and there, clusters of fledgling bhakti yogin were sitting in the mud chanting, and families of picnickers, who had scoured the park for scrub and kindling that morning, were roasting up lunches of hot dogs, marshmallows, and banana skins. From the thick, bare branches of a nearby oak, where a number of beings were enjoying a quiet, telescopic view of the proceedings, the meadow looked a little like an action painting that had just been splashed onto the landscape by a crazy Brobdingnagian.

Ginsberg entered the picture with his hair flying and his cymbals clattering, scrambling out of reach of a following of panting celebrants. In the last few hours he had managed to have a hike in the snow in Canada, where he had been reading that weekend, make two plane connections for the city, drop off his knapsack and snowshoes on Tenth Street, collect his orderly's suit, and maneuver his way to the park through some forty blocks of Easter Parade; and, consequently, he was somewhat unnerved by the sudden show of admiration. He had tried hollering at the celebrants—"Hey, let me alone! Go make your *own* scene! Why in God's name don't you people go have a good time?"—but by the time he found his friends, who had staked out a small circle of mud in the middle of the meadow, there were at least a hundred poetry lovers chasing him.

Ginsberg's friends had just lit a pile of incense sticks, and they were holding a boisterous Easter kirtan around their fire. Maretta was there in her culottes and a new length of gauze, warbling along in a piercing tremulo and looking extremely refreshed from a second pilgrimage to the lamasary in southern

New Jersey. Orlovsky, who had elected to spend a pious Easter
Sunday purifying the apartment, was at home with two
family-size bottles of Ajax Liquid which he bought on sale at the
corner *bodega*, but Corso had come to the Be-In as his envoy,
gloomily sporting a tattered purple velvet jacket and an enormous,
clanking Maltese cross. Corso, who was making mud pies at the
moment, was wedged into the circle between Maretta and
Beelzebub. A skinny young man with rolling black eyes and a
waxed mustache, Beelzebub had recently signed a contract for
two weeks' work in a sado-masochistic underground extrava-
ganza, and today he was dressed, in keeping with his status as
a film star, in fancy sunglasses, a pair of fawn-colored stretch
pants, a turtleneck sweater, and a several strands of dazzling Siva
beads. Having prepared himself for the festivities with an in-
vigorating dose of pills, Beelzebub was chanting—much to the
dismay of Corso, whom he kept bumping into on his down beats
—with equal theatricality. Another one of Ginsberg's old board-
ers, the woodsman from the Eighth Street Bookstore, was sitting
in the circle with his girl friend. And so was Kumwar Kumar, the
Sanskrit professor from Columbia who had initiated Ginsberg
and Maretta into Siva worship several weeks ago. Kumar
had come to the Be-In with a date and a sitar teacher, and he
was sitting between them, in a trance, leading the kirtan, when
Ginsberg lowered himself carefully into the mud. It was two in
the afternoon. Ginsberg warmed up with a few long *"Oms"* and
began to sing.

Six hours later, Ginsberg and his friends, who were still singing, were in a plush-carpeted private elevator on their way to the
forty-fourth floor of the New York Hilton Hotel. They had left
the Be-In together after the sun set, and had been enjoying high
tea and Oreo cookies with a group of genial, aging Dadaists in a
blackened garret just across Central Park West in the Dakota,
when someone slipped in, tacked a note to the door, and

disappeared. The note, which was eventually discovered and examined by the light of a dripping violet candle, turned out to be an invitation to a party at the West Penthouse of the hotel. No one knew who the host was, but it was observed that the tea and the cookies were running out. The garret was empty in a matter of a few minutes. Walking over to the Hilton, Ginsberg and his friends had stopped the traffic on Sixth Avenue with their spirited exorcism of demons, and now, in the elevator, they were barreling through a polysyllabic Sanskrit mantra—it was the longest Sanskrit mantra in Ginsberg's repertoire —for the purpose of evenly distributing blessings throughout the hotel. The mantra happened to last exactly as long as the elevator ride. This was taken as a coincidence by Corso, but by Ginsberg as a promising sign.

A chubby little man in a blue suit was standing at the elevator, with his hand out, when the door slid open, and the final, booming "de" of the mantra filled the penthouse. At least a dozen celebrants swept by him, clanging their cymbals and uttering cries of delight at the outsized oriental splendors of his suite. Corso, Maretta, Beelzebub and some ladies from the tea party bounded up a spiral staircase in the middle of a vast foyer to inspect the bedrooms. Corso planted himself at a Louis XV desk in a gold room of Acropoline proportions and, commanding a god's-eye view of Central Park, immediately began telephoning friends to let them in on his unlikely whereabouts. Maretta and one of the ladies—a fellow Tibetan Buddhist, as it happened—came upon a marble bathroom, with eighteen-karat fixtures on the plumbing, and sat down on the rim of the tub to pray. Beelzebub, across the hall in a bedroom of comparable brilliance, ran around opening the doors to massive chinoiserie armoires which had television sets and stereo speakers hidden inside them, while two more of the ladies searched in vain for the controls of an adjoining sauna bath.

Downstairs, their host stood with his hand out, staring at the beings as they scattered over the apartment. Then he reached into the back pocket of his trousers, pulled out a crumpled handkerchief, and mopped his forehead. Ginsberg, who had been waiting in the foyer, walked over cheerfully and introduced himself.

"Groovy pad you've got here," Ginsberg said.

The man smiled weakly. "The name's Malina, but you can call me Sam, I guess," he said.

"You can call me Allen," Ginsberg said.

"Say, you're the one I wanted to meet." Malina blushed. He said that he had just been browsing through his favorite magazine, *Status-Diplomat*, and would really love to have Ginsberg's opinion, as a writer, on that fine piece in the latest issue entitled "The Absolute Necessity of Owning Thirteen Rolls Royces." He looked unhappy when Ginsberg answered, "*Status-what?*", but as soon as the poet, who had spotted a life-sized gilded Buddha in the distance, asked to be shown around, Malina brightened considerably.

Malina took Ginsberg by the elbow and steered him out of the foyer and into a room which he referred to as the grand salon. The room was roughly seventy-by-forty feet. It had a wall of glass with a view out over Manhattan and well into the Bronx, Queens, Westchester, and New Jersey, and it housed—along with the Buddha, which Beelzebub later identified as Bangkok Decadent—two gigantic Cambodian temple rubbings, a baroque coffee table the width of a highway intersection, and a big black concert-grand piano, as well as a scattering of twelve-foot orange couches, Chinese lamps, and American plastic crocks full of chopped chicken liver. A number of extremely sleek people were gliding across an expanse of pale carpeting, sipping out of snifters. Two more elevator loads of hippies were heading for the crocks.

Malina, winding up the tour behind a long bar backed by a Japanese tea screen, said that the West Penthouse, which he liked to rent on his business trips from Cincinnati, cost him five hundred dollars a day plus tax, but that the chopped chicken liver, which he had ordered especially for the hippies, was not included in the price.

Ginsberg looked up from the bar, where he was mixing a drink with all kinds of improvised, enthusiastic flourishes, and peered at Malina. "Hey, what kind of business is that?" Ginsberg said.

"You might say the business of investment," Malina said, leaning forward confidentially. "See that man near the statue? He's my partner—but he's really more what you might call a front man. Jim's good at *people*."

Ginsberg thought for a minute and then said, "Say, you might be able to help me out. Like I've gotten really interested in the military-industrial complex—you know, like who's really making the bread off the war, and like who controls things—"

"Put your money with Dillon," Malina whispered. "He's very big. Kennedy got very healthy with Dillon. He put ten million in the market with Dillon in 'sixty-two, and now his estate is in excess of forty million dollars."

Ginsberg called to his friend Jack Smith, who had just walked in, to say that the Kennedys were in on a piece of United Fruit. Smith nodded, knowingly, and then sank like a languishing *Firebird* into the depths of an orange couch. He was a rather imposing addition to the Hilton—tall, weedy, pallid to the point of imminent demise, and dressed in a velvet Elizabethan court suit with mutton sleeves and a big starched ruff. There was a ring of undoubtably exotic and even ghastly origin on every one of Smith's long, pointed fingers. Strange jewels hung from his earlobes. And his eyes, which were rimmed with soot, had been extended into sweeping, deep blue wings. Malina, who was speechless, stared at him.

"Boy, this is some party," Malina said, finally, taking the drink that Ginsberg had been holding out to him. "I can't wait to see the rest of the cast."

Ginsberg shook his head. "I'm a little curious—like why did you invite us?" he said.

Malina pointed across the room to one of the sleek people, a young man who was juggling a number of female guests with what appeared to be complete success. "I asked *him*," Malina said. "Duryea is our all-round man-on-the-spot. I said to him, 'Duryea Jones, no *In* people—I want some *Out* people tonight.' " Malina sighed. "Yesterday it was the Burtons. I'm tired of In people," he said.

Ginsberg picked up his cymbals from the bar. "Well, see you," he said. "I'm going to chant. Want to join us?"

"Oh, no! That is, thank's anyway, I'm what you might call more of a *listener*," Malina explained, backing off. "Would you believe *listening?*" As soon as Ginsberg was settled down on the carpet, chanting with Kumar, the sitar teacher, and the woodsman's girl friend, Malina motioned to the man called Duryea Jones. Jones came trotting over. A paisley handkerchief was flopping carelessly from the breast pocket of his fiitted English suit.

"I think we've got a very hip group tonight," Malina congratulated his all-round man-on-the-spot. "You did a fine job."

"He's a very unusual talent—Ginsberg," Jones said.

Malina beamed.

"Yes, and he's interesting, too," Jones went on. "And entertaining. Didn't I tell you he'd be entertaining?"

The two men stood together for a moment, appreciating the mantra to Krishna as a young cowpoke. Beelzebub, who had just slid down the banister of the spiral staircase, spotted them.

"Man, listen to that chant," Beelzebub shouted, grabbing Malina by the shoulders and giving him a hot, apocalyptic stare. "There is power in intonation, man. Like did you ever really *feel* the creative and destructive power of the voice before?"

Malina shook his head.

Jones moved in quickly, but before he could say a word, Beelzebub had thrown himself onto the carpet and was stretched out flat on his back, beating time with his head.

"Isn't it awful?" Malina whispered happily to Jones.

By ten that night, the grand salon was mobbed. Ginsberg and his friends had run through "Gopala Gopala Devaka Nandina Gopala," "Sri Ram Jai Ram Jai Jai Ram," and "Hare Krishna," and were now in the middle of a command performance of the "Prajna Paramita Sutra." Over at the concert grand, the vice-president of a downtown brokerage house was tinkling through a medley from *Hello Dolly* for a stately Indian in a black turban and a French model in a satin pants suit. And, next to them, Corso and a hotel owner in a yachting blazer and sharkskin slacks were somewhat embroiled in an aesthetic dispute. The hotel man, whose name was Herman, was contemplating Corso with a congealed sneer. He had just called him a filthy beatnik, and, at the moment, he was waiting for Corso's reply.

Corso was thinking. At last he said, "What you are, Herman, is mean."

The model and the Indian turned around.

"I want you to meet this nice man—he's involved in hotels," Corso, who had just spotted the model, said.

The model confronted Herman's fake tan and carefully waved gray hair with a cool but admiring silence. Herman put his hand on the back of her neck.

"This wise guy says he writes poetry," Herman said. "I can't believe it."

"Go ahead, tell him I write poetry," Corso told the model.

"He is quite a well-known poet, I believe," the Indian said.

"It's just not *right*," Herman said. He was steering the model, by the neck, toward one of the orange couches, and he asked her in a sexy, confidential voice, "When do *you* think was the last time that beatnik had a shower?"

"I don't like you any more, Herman—I'm leaving," Corso said. He made a scary face and then stalked off in the direction of the bar. The model, arranging herself on the couch in a fetching demi-recline, watched him, smiling.

"He is amusing, *non?*" she murmured to Herman.

"You like him, you take him home and sleep with him," Herman said.

The model yawned.

Herman edged toward her. "What are you doing here, anyway, with all these dirty men?" he began again. "You look like a nice girl. You could have great opportunities, a nice girl like you." He paused, philosophically. "Tell me, dear, aren't you shocked by all this?"

"Ah, *oui*, but of course," the model said.

Herman was elated. "Well, I've seen the same thing in the East," he went on, pointing at Ginsberg, who had gotten up off the floor and was dancing around the coffee table, waving his arms. "It's a Gomorrah in the East. It's corrupt. You can take it from me." Herman was sliding his hand across the couch toward the model's knee.

"Hi," Ginsberg said, plopping down between them. "I saw you calling me."

Herman glared, nursing his hand.

"What's your name?" Ginsberg said.

"Herman," Herman said. "I know *you.*"

"What's your *last* name?" Ginsberg said.

Herman muttered his last name. "I just had the pleasure of meeting another one of your leaders," he said. "There he is now —he's putting his drink on the rug just like it was *ground.*" Ginsberg looked up and waved at Corso, across the room.

"Where are you from, Herman?" Ginsberg said.

"New Jersey," Herman said. "I'm a Jewish boy from New Jersey."

"I'm a Jewish boy from New Jersey too," Ginsberg said cheerfully.

"I know all about you," Herman cut in. "I've read all about you people in *Time, Life,* and *Look.*"

"Do you think you can get a good picture of people that way?" Ginsberg asked him.

Herman took off his glasses and rubbed his eyes. "I don't know. I'm just a businessman."

"I bet I earn more money than you do," Ginsberg said, grinning.

Herman blanched. "How much?" he said.

Ginsberg leaned over and cupped his hand on Herman's ear. "Sometimes a few hundred a week," he whispered.

"*I* make three quarters of a million a year," Herman said. He tossed a broad smile to the model, who was swishing her brandy around.

Ginsberg sighed. "Well, Herman, what do you think of all the beatniks here?" he said.

"I'm frank," Herman said. "I'll tell you honestly. I wouldn't have them in my house."

"Why not?" Ginsberg said, making a vague gesture that included his friends. Beelzebub, on the floor, was chatting with a reporter from the *Wall Street Journal* about an old guru of his who was the fourteenth incarnation of a flying llama from Tibet. Maretta, across the room, was draped over a chaise longue, smoking. Kumar and his sitar teacher were still singing. Smith hadn't moved in three-quarters of an hour, and Corso was complaining to Malina because all of the chopped chicken liver had been mysteriously removed.

"They seem pretty well behaved," Ginsberg said.

"Look, I'm not a stranger to all this," Herman said crossly. "I have a big apartment on Thirteenth Street. That's in Greenwich Village."

Ginsberg said that he was acquainted with the Village.

"And I can tell you," Herman went on, "they wouldn't get into my building." He thought for a minute. "My living room— it's not as big as this is, but it has a fireplace that works," he said.

"Groovy," Ginsberg said. "Like I don't have a fireplace."

Herman changed the subject. "You people are so dirty," he said. "I tell you the flood in Florence did less damage than you people would have."

"You dig Florence?" Ginsberg asked him, slipping off his shoes and kicking them under the couch.

"I love Florence," Herman said. "Of all the cities in the world, Florence has taken me most into its—its *bosom*." Then he said, "No, definitely not in *my* building. At least until they had taken showers. Tell me, do you think showers would do any good?"

"Hey, that's not fair—they take showers," Ginsberg said.

"And I say they're dirty," Herman said. "*I* took a bath tonight. I washed *my* feet."

Herman was staring at Ginsberg's feet, one of which was burrowing under a cushion near him.

"I washed my feet tonight," Ginsberg said.

Flinching slightly, Herman examined the foot. "It doesn't look it," Herman said.

"Well, I *did*," Ginsberg said. He sat back, studying his foot for a moment, and then he poked Herman. "What time did *you* take a bath?" he said.

"It was seven o'clock tonight," Herman replied.

Ginsberg was delighted. "I washed *my* feet at eight o'clock tonight," he said.

"Where?" Herman snapped.

Ginsberg looked up slyly. "At a tea party at the Dakota. So there, Herman."

"So there, so you *didn't* take a bath—it was just your feet," Herman said.

"I took a bath this morning, in Canada." Ginsberg grinned.

"In Canada?" Herman checked himself. "Do you know where you are?" he said. "What are you doing in this beautiful place? What is it you people want?"

"Just a peaceful world, with like everybody running around having a good time," Ginsberg said. "*Spiritual* things."

The model yawned again.

Herman, however, sat up straight. "I have a spiritual problem myself," he said. "I'm trying to decide whether to get married again."

"That's *your* spiritual problem," Ginsberg said. "Do you love her?"

"She has more money than me," Herman said. "She's my equal."

Ginsberg pointed to Maretta, who had fallen asleep on the chaise longue, with one leg up and her other leg dangling over the edge. The hem of her new gauze shawl had settled into an abandoned glass of Scotch.

"Do you see that girl over there?" Ginsberg said proudly. "She's *my* girl friend."

"Oh," Herman said.

"She speaks Tibetan," Ginsberg added.

"My girl friend only speaks English," Herman said.

Ginsberg patted the hotel man on the head. "Are you happy, Herman?"

"I don't know." Herman shrugged. "I have money and a nice apartment."

"And a girl friend with more money than you," Ginsberg said.

"And children," Herman added. "A girl twenty—"

"Does she read my poetry?" Ginsberg said.

"I wouldn't know," Herman said. "I don't speak to her. My girl friend speaks to her, though." Herman paused. "Do you think what you write is beautiful?"

"Yes," Ginsberg said.

A moment later, Herman was alone with the model again. Someone had started shouting, "Mr. Ginsberg! *Please*, Mr. Ginsberg," and Ginsberg had jumped up and circled the room until he spotted Malina, by the door to the foyer, frantically beckoning.

"Do something," Malina groaned. "For God's sake *do* something."

"Do what?" Ginsberg said.

Malina stamped his foot. "Make them stop. Make them go home." He waved helplessly in the direction of the spiral staircase. "They're all up *there*," he said. "They've been making phone calls. They've called Japan. Would you believe *Japan?*"

Ginsberg blocked a grin. "That's not very nice," he said.

Maretta, who had just awakened, flew past them and up the staircase to explore. She was back in seconds.

"He's locked every fucking door," Maretta said.

"It's *his* penthouse," Ginsberg told her. "He can lock the doors if he wants to."

"It wasn't *every* door," Malina said. "Just *three* doors. Just the doors to rooms with telephones."

"Man, I can't even get to the bathroom," Maretta said.

"And they've canceled dinner," Corso added, walking up to them. He was still looking for the chopped liver.

Ginsberg turned to Malina. "Is that true?" he said. "Like the sign said we were invited for dinner."

"I learned it from the m-a-i-d," Corso said, drawing himself up and fixing Malina with one of his fierce, Gilgamesh looks.

Malina ran to the bar, where he began hiding bottles of brandy and Scotch. Ginsberg followed him.

"Look, I admire you, Mr. Ginsberg—you're a beautiful man," Malina whispered. His arms were full of Courvoisier VSOP. "I just don't understand all the consternation here. There doesn't have to *be* all this consternation. People like you—like *us*—we're beautiful."

"Tell me what happened," Ginsberg said gently.

"I've disconnected all the phones," Malina began. "Can't you make them go?"

Ginsberg shrugged. "I'll try," he said, and then, "Just tell them to go. It's your party. Just say, 'The party's over.'"

"I can't," Malina cried. "I don't know how to talk to them. They won't listen to me. They'll listen to you."

Ginsberg put his arm around Malina. "Look," he said. "What's so scary about these kids? If they've like displeased you, you just say like, 'Good night.' Or say, 'What the fuck do you mean, abusing my hospitality!' Say *some*thing."

Malina shook his head.

"Do whatever is your pleasure," Ginsberg said.

"What does that mean—my pleasure?" Malina said quietly.

"Don't you know?" Ginsberg said.

About the Author

JANE KRAMER is *The New Yorker*'s European correspondent and writes the "Letter from Europe" for the magazine. She is the author of seven other books, most recently *Whose Art Is It?*, which in its original form won the National Magazine Award in 1993. She won a 1981 National Book Award for *The Last Cowboy*. *Europeans* was nominated for a National Book Critics Circle Award, and in 1993 made her the first American, and the first woman, to win the *Prix Europeen de l'Essai Charles Veillon*. She is married to the anthropologist Vincent Crapanzano, and they have a daughter, Aleksandra. Jane Kramer lives in Paris and New York.